CONTENTS

YOU, THE FANS, HELP ME FEEL CONFIDENT. I'LL CONTINUE TO GIVE MY ALL FOR YOU...

WHEN you arrive at a club, for the fans to then back you after just a few days there, to the point where you feel real love and affection from them, that's just amazing. It's surprising too, because I know it doesn't happen at every club.

The best thing for a player when he is out there on the field is to feel full of confidence. And, along with the confidence and trust of my team-mates, the support the fans have given me here at Liverpool has been incredible.

My big dream was to come here and play for Liverpool. Immediately I had a good feeling about the club. It's great when the manager backs you to the hilt right from the start, your team-mates go out of their way to help you and the fans themselves help you, stick with you, really like you. That's really good.

I think the fans here play a major role, bigger than at other clubs. They really appreciate the players and applaud if we try something. That's what makes a player feel confident. It's a really positive thing and gives you even more belief.

The song the fans sing about me is another example of the brilliant welcome I've had. People have explained it to me but I don't fully understand it yet. To tell the truth I'm still surprised when people start singing it, and by the number of people who sing it. Maybe it means I am doing my job well. All I can say is thanks to everyone for such great support and I'll continue to give my all.

This is the story of my life and career so far and I hope you enjoy it.

CREDITS

Photographic Credits:	Trinity Mirror, Getty Images, PA Pics, Imagery © Liverpool Football Club & Athletic Grounds Ltd
Executive Editor:	Ken Rogers
Senior Editor:	Steve Hanrahan
Senior Art Editor:	Rick Cooke
Senior Production Ed:	Paul Dove
Magazine Editor:	Roy Gilfoyle
Writers:	Chris McLoughlin, John Hynes, William Hughes, Simon Hughes
Designers:	Colin Sumpter, Alison Barkley, Lisa Critchley, Michael Perry
Cover Design:	Jamie Dunmore

© Published in Great Britain in 2011 by Trinity Mirror Sport Media, PO Box 48, Old Hall Street, Liverpool L69 3EB.

The uarez story

'I KEEP SHIRTS FROM IMPORTANT MOMENTS IN MY CAREER. HOPEFULLY I WILL HAVE A LOT MORE TO KEEP IN THE FUTURE WITH LIVERPOOL, AND SOME MEDALS TOO'

Interview: John Hynes

A crowded space, with people all around. Others might be hesitant. Luis Suarez isn't. He's at ease in such situations. We've all seen him twist and turn in incredible fashion to create a goal or a chance on the football field.

This time he's just entered the Melwood press room, where Kenny Dalglish regularly enjoys his verbal jousts with the media.

There are various parties waiting in the room to speak to the Uruguayan. He greets each with a smile before shaking hands with the interpreter and starting to chat.

It's a surprisingly warm morning in October, 2011. Liverpool's number seven has been at the club for nine months. Often players arriving from a different league understandably need time to acclimatise. For the Uruguayan his adaptation seemed effortless.

A goal on his debut against Stoke City, a reworking of Depeche Mode's 'Just Can't Get Enough' in honour of him and being likened to club legend Kenny Dalglish. They are just three examples of how he has already become a hero.

Speaking to John Hynes, Suarez exclusively answers questions about his life and career so far, his smooth transition to his new world in Liverpool, plus his goal celebrations and hopes for the future.

As a kid growing up in Uruguay were you aware of LFC?
Yes and I'm not saying it because I'm playing here now, but as a kid I always loved to play as Liverpool on the PlayStation. If we play now and I am Liverpool it's more for a laugh because I'm actually in the team, but back then I would always choose Liverpool.

Who did you support?
I supported Nacional and then played for them.

Like most kids, you obviously played a lot of football. Do you remember getting your first pair of boots?
I played in bare feet a lot as a kid. I don't remember my first pair of boots. The boots that I remember the most are not any that I have bought for myself but a pair that my wife Sofia got me as a present when I was only 17.

She was living and working in Barcelona at the time and earned the money to buy me this special pair that I liked a lot and had always really wanted.

I was wearing them when Nacional won the league. I scored a lot of goals in them too. They brought me a lot of good luck and I have kept them to this day. Sofia was my girlfriend back then

and she worked hard to buy me those boots.

You come from a large family don't you?
Yes. My dad's name is Rodolfo and my mum is called Sandra. He lives in Salto, where I was born, 500km from Montevideo. My mum lives in Montevideo and she has a bakery. They're separated, my mum has remarried and my dad has a partner but they are not married.

They have both worked hard over the years and are now semi-retired and taking things a bit easier.

What about brothers and sisters?
My mum's little boy Facundo is the youngest, and he is seven, nearly eight. Diego is 19, Maxi is 23, Leticia is 27 and Giovanna is 28 or 29, I can't remember. And finally Paolo, who is 31. Maxi was a better player than me but he doesn't even play nowadays.

Tell us about Salto and Montevideo.
Salto is quite a way from the capital and, for me, as for many people, aside from Montevideo, Salto and its surrounding province is the nicest place in Uruguay. It has some lovely places to visit and

A young Luis Suarez with team-mates Maarten Stekelenburg and Klaas-Jan Huntelaar and Ajax fans

the people are very down to earth and are always there to help you. I just always feel sorry that I have never had a chance to really enjoy such a beautiful city, having left at such a young age. I was only seven when I moved to Montevideo.

You were still a teenager when you left Nacional to join Groningen in Holland. It must have been difficult to leave home for a new club in Europe?
Yes it was a little bit tough to begin with. The manager wanted me to do more training. He showed me what I needed to work on on the training ground as well as giving advice on how I should play in games. He also did lots of other things that were a great help to me.

The success you had there – 15 goals in 37 games and helping the team qualify for the UEFA Cup – led to you joining Ajax. Did going to the biggest club in Holland put extra pressure on you?
There was a little bit [more pressure] there but I really loved playing for Ajax. I felt very comfortable and happy there, and that was down to the people and the team.

They are a big club, respected

by everyone. So you always went into every game setting out to win it. I learned a lot in my time at Ajax, including how to fine-tune the many things in my game that needed some attention.

What was the most important thing you learnt from playing in Holland?
I learned that I needed to be much more professional. I realised in terms of preparation I had to do everything totally differently off the field compared to how it was done back in Uruguay.

There weren't as many pre-match get-togethers, so you learn to take responsibility for yourself and what you eat and drink. Here in Europe you know that you should stop drinking Coke, and that you should drink plenty of water because it's good for you or you shouldn't eat as much bread, all the things you just didn't even realise in Uruguay. At home the team gets together the night before every single game, but not here or in Holland. In Europe, you suddenly realise just exactly what it is like to be a professional footballer.

In that time you've also become a regular in the Uruguay team. The side finished fourth at the World Cup before winning the 2011 Copa

America. How has this success been achieved?
The main person responsible for this is the coach, Mr Tabarez. For me he is the man who started everything, and he is the architect of all the success that Uruguay has enjoyed in recent years because he is a very straight-talking coach who sees the long-term picture and builds for the future.

What were your realistic expectations for you and the team going in to the World Cup?
I think that in our heads we thought we could qualify from our group. It had been so long since Uruguay had reached the latter stages so the idea was to enjoy the experience, because it was the World Cup after all.

Fan favourite Luis gets a club award at Ajax, and helps coach some youngsters

We were determined to enjoy our moment on the big stage, aware of the fact that for some of us, it might be our one chance to play in a World Cup. I think that this was the best way Uruguay could have approached the tournament, quietly confident that we could perform well but at the same time staying under the radar as we were not one of everyone's fancied teams.

Reaching the semi-finals in South Africa obviously raised expectations for the Copa. Did that make the tournament more difficult?
I think that the same group of players have been together now over the last four years and we all know each other very well, so we were confident that

'I really loved playing for Ajax. I felt very comfortable and happy there, and that was down to the people and the team. They are a big club, respected by everyone'

we could give a very good account of ourselves in the tournament.

That was important for the team, a real plus, believing that we had a real chance of winning the trophy. The other important thing was that we managed to close our ears to all the pre-tournament talk about Uruguay. Doing otherwise would have been bad. So I think the squad's mental approach to the Copa America was ideal.

After the triumph what kind of reception did the squad receive when they got home?
When we arrived back home at two in the morning it was all very emotional as we drove by on the open-top bus. I was really moved by the fact that there were so many people out to greet us, from elderly people to little children, people who hadn't enjoyed the success of the national side for a long time.

There were kids of eleven who had never seen Uruguay as champions of a big tournament. It truly was a beautiful moment, very emotional, and as a fan of Uruguay myself when I was growing up as a boy who loved his football, I could understand how they were feeling. That made it all the more enjoyable for me.

Can you walk down the street in Uruguay now?
No, it's very difficult for me to do it.

Clearly you are enjoying your football with Uruguay and Liverpool. How have you settled in to life on Merseyside?
My family are very happy and content here, both my wife and my daughter. We spend a lot of time at home. For example, after a game we sometimes go home and cook some food on the barbecue.

No-one has ever treated us anything but nicely. Whenever we go out for a walk or if we go out for a meal, everyone is really respectful

Suarez celebrates scoring in the Copa America final against Paraguay

and polite, which is great, and that's why you are made to feel happy and very much at ease here. There have been no problems with either sets of supporters!

Foreign players often mention food and weather when they come to England. How have you found those elements of the UK?
I have always eaten the same food wherever I go, I never change, so that's not been a problem. I sometimes get food sent over from Uruguay but I buy plenty of the food here too.

And the weather, it's the same as I've been used to for a while now,

Quick Question with Luis Suarez...

DOES THE CHALLENGE OF HELPING LIVERPOOL GET BACK TO THE TOP OF EUROPEAN FOOTBALL EXCITE YOU?

"I'm very excited about the future here at Liverpool. The club has a long and glorious history and is respected by football supporters, not just in Europe but across the whole world. The people here have the passion and determination to take Liverpool back to where it should be.

"I have been in Europe for several seasons now and it seems every season Liverpool has been challenging for the most important European competitions. I understand they haven't won the domestic title for a long time but there is a real desire amongst the people here to make sure that doesn't continue for too much longer. I want to be a part of that."

'My family are very happy and content here, both my wife and my daughter. We spend a lot of time at home. No-one has ever treated us anything but nicely'

so there's no problem there either. I always think that if you are happy off the field, you always show it when you are on the field.

Have any of your family been to visit you?
I've had two nephews over from Uruguay. They came to have a look around and pay us a visit. We've also had my wife's family over from Spain, as they live in Barcelona and it's much easier to get here.

We've still not had anyone else over from Uruguay because it's quite difficult to organise as they are all working. Our nieces and nephews are busy in school.

How often do you speak to people back home?
All the time, usually on the phone or by text messaging.

You seem to have a variety of celebrations after each goal. Are they dedicated to your friends and family?
They always just come out automatically, without planning them. The one where I kiss just here [kisses his wrist], that's for my little girl. Kissing my ring is for my wife. But this one where I shoot like this [makes pistols with each hand], it

just happens, I don't plan that one! I almost don't realise I'm doing it, it's automatic.

Do you have any pre-match superstitions?
I have one or two but I would prefer not to say what they are.

Do you keep all of your shirts, match-balls, etc?
When I score three goals or if it's

Luis kisses his wrist or his wedding ring to pay tribute to his daughter and wife

an important game I always keep something like a shirt. For example I have kept the first shirt I wore here, from my debut against Stoke City. Other times I've kept a shirt when I got a hat-trick with Ajax or when I've scored in games back in Uruguay, I've got them from the World Cup and Copa America games also. Hopefully I will have a lot more stuff to keep in the future with Liverpool, and some medals too.

'Celebrations just come out automatically, without planning them. It just happens. I almost don't realise what I'm doing!'

MAKING A NAME FOR HIMSELF

In the first of four instalments throughout this unique souvenir edition, we take a look at Luis Suarez's amazing rise to prominence, starting with his early years in his native Uruguay as his boyhood dream of being a footballer began to take shape...

S ALTO in Uruguay's far western frontier is just a river and a bridge away from Argentina. Lonely Planet says that travellers should only see the town for two reasons – to visit the nearby hot springs at Dayman or to pass through it en route to Concordia over the border.

"It is a sleepy place where not much happens," says journalist Luis Inzaurralde from the El Observador newspaper. In the shop storefronts that align its main street, imaginatively named Uruguay, old men in Panama hats spend most of the day sipping on *mate* (a local herbal tea), holding service on the issues that affect them most.

The town has no professional football team but it is proud of the fact that it has provided the current national side with two of its star strikers.

Born within 21 days of one another, Napoli's lank-haired Edinson Cavani is the younger of the two. He moved to Montevideo when he was 12 years old and later emerged through the youth system at Danubio before transferring to Italy and hitting the goal trail initially with Palermo.

The first son of 1987 followed a similar route to Europe. Liverpool's Luis Suarez and his family re-located to the capital when Luis

was just seven. There, his father worked at a small factory that made pasta and his mother combined her job as a housekeeper while taking care of her seven children.

There were times of struggle just like there are in any family, but, the Suarez clan lived a comfortable life. "We were not poor, but we were certainly not rich either," Suarez recalled. "As you can imagine coming from a large family, we did not have many resources at home, which meant we had to carry on with a very normal life, full of sacrifices. But we were all happy."

Uruguay was the only country in the Americas which did not go into recession as a result of the financial crisis which started to envelop world business in 2009 – the same year when its government initiated a policy which means that the country became the first in the world to provide every school child with a free laptop and wireless internet.

Montevideo was first to benefit, "as it always does," Inzaurralde says – but this is no surprise given that it is one of the most magnetic capital cities in the world for attracting its population. This is also reflected in football. Of the 16 teams in its top 'national' league, 15 are based in the city with only Tacuarembo defying the odds with a lonely

Luis started to make a name for himself at youth level with Nacional before breaking into the first-team

>>

Hero:
Gabriel
Batistuta

existence in the far north of the country.

'Many of the countries in the continent [South America] are extremely centralised – the legacy of a colonial economic past whereby raw materials were exported and manufactured products brought in,' wrote Tim Vickery in World Soccer magazine. 'Typically, the port where this trade took place grew into a capital city (in this case Montevideo), which lorded it over an underdeveloped hinterland. As football is the game of the city, this domination is reflected in the way that the major teams tend to be clustered together in the capital.'

With so many teams within a close proximity to watch, Suarez and his brothers started taking football more seriously. "I started playing football when I was very young and by the age of four I would run faster with the ball than without it," Suarez said. Such talent led to an invitation at the age of 11 to a national youth training camp in La Plata, Argentina, but he had to turn down the offer.

"All my dreams had come true but it was too expensive so I had to decline because I didn't even have enough money to buy a pair of shoes," he added.

Inspired by Argentine striker, Gabriel Batistuta, Suarez – at 14 – caught the eye of Montevideo's (and the country's) second most successful side, Nacional.

"He [Batistuta] was a complete number nine," Suarez said. "Brave, skilful – powerful. What I liked most was that he could score goals from anywhere. When I was a child and he scored for Fiorentina, I would play on the street and try to repeat what I had seen. Importantly, he was a hard worker who never had it easy. I could relate to that."

Suarez also took inspiration from his older

brother, Paolo, who six years his senior started his career in Montevideo with Basanez before playing for a host of clubs in Central America and Colombia.

"Paolo made his professional debut just around the time I started with Nacional," Suarez remembered. "He is a midfielder and better technically than me. His success gave me hope that it was possible to fulfil your dreams if you work hard enough."

Aged 15, Suarez admits that he wasn't working hard enough and after partying until the early hours one morning, he was given an ultimatum by his youth team coach. "Either you train like your team-mates or I will never pick you again," came the warning.

The advice was heeded. Within a year he was part of the first-team squad and on May 3 2005 he made his Nacional debut against Junior de Barranquilla in the Copa Libertadores (South America's version of the European Champions League). The pressure to perform was immediate. Although Nacional had won the Libertedores on three previous occasions, their last title was in 1988. No Uruguayan club had even reached the semi-finals since 1989.

Domestically, too, Nacional were in a state of flux. Despite having won 43 league titles to Penarol's 46, suddenly the monopoly had come to an end (from the start of the professional era in 1932 until 1986 the Montevideo giants had won the championship on all but two occasions). In 1987, the title went to Defensor, followed by Danubio the next year, Progreso in '89, Bella Vista in '90 and Defensor again in '91.

By the time Suarez made his debut in '05, Nacional had reversed this trend, winning the title another five times. The manner of the teams that had claimed them, however, had changed – Nacional's squad made up mainly

Early years:
A young Luis
strikes a pose

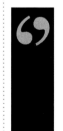

BY THE AGE OF FOUR I WOULD RUN FASTER WITH THE BALL THAN WITHOUT IT

>>

of ageing players with experience of playing abroad and youngsters at the very beginning of their careers.

The global market had opened up and with a population of just 3.4 million, it became just as impossible for Nacional and Penarol to keep their best players in their prime as it was to sign the best from smaller clubs who were now more likely just to head straight to Europe or elsewhere in South America where increased wages proved an attraction.

Last year, a survey revealed that in spite of its relatively small population Uruguay has sent overseas almost as many players as Brazil and Argentina that have significantly larger populations, 180 and 40 million. The main destination for most Uruguayan players between 2000 and 2010 had been neighbouring Argentina with 238 professionals followed by Mexico with 113, Italy, 112 and Spain 102. The diaspora led to a decrease in standards in Uruguay's domestic competitions.

A focus on youth development pioneered by national coach Oscar Washington Tabarez led to raised standards from under-17s to under-20 level and Suarez was a part of this.

"The first thing that struck me and a lot of other people was the way he [Suarez] used his body strength to back into people – like the way Kenny Dalglish used to for Liverpool," Tim Vickery said. "He was brilliant with his back to goal, protecting the ball. If you can do that at 17 in a ruthless league like the Uruguayan Primera Division you know

Luis with his young Nacional team-mates

there is something special about the player. Nacional were fully aware of his talent and they appreciated that soon enough he'd be moving on."

Within months of his debut, Brazilian side Flamengo were rumoured to be preparing a bid, which, if placed, would have forced Nacional to sell. Suarez, though, remained focused and went on to play a key role in the clinching of another league title (his first) in 2006, scoring 12 goals in 29 games.

"Suarez was the key to that team," Vickery added. "They had a lot of experience in key areas but Suarez provided that spark needed to win matches when it mattered.

"It was only a matter of time before he moved to Europe."

Oscar Washington Tabarez helped develop young talent like Suarez in Uruguay

Coates: Nacional gave us perfect grounding

IF there is one place in the world other than Italy where defending is regarded as an art rather than a necessity, then it is on the banks of the River Plate.

The appreciation began in 1950s Argentina – a time when strikers reigned; scores were high, bonuses were handed to the most prolific of marksmen and the club moneymen, ever reluctant. Over time, ways were devised to stop the drain.

Estudiantes from the port city of La Plata were the first side not to just embrace defending but celebrate it as a route to winning matches. By the 60s stoppers like Ramon Aguirre Suarez and Raul Madero were notorious: urbane and charming off the field, but as calculated as a team of gothic prison guards on it.

The approach bore success and consecutive managers followed the formula. When Estudiantes played Manchester United in the 1968 Intercontinental Cup, the consequences were brutal. The shin-pad-splitting fouls were brazen but the Argentines won, so it didn't matter. To them, it was a necessary means to achieving respect on the world stage. "We enjoyed this reputation," Suarez later said. "It defined our identity."

Over the estuary in the Uruguayan capital of Montevideo, attitudes were influenced by Jose Santamaria, the most elegantly remorseless of centre-backs. After beginning his career with Nacional, he moved to Real Madrid in 1957 and promptly won three European Cups. Later, he followed the lead of his team-mate, Alfredo Di Stefano by representing Spain rather than his homeland.

It is said that Santamaria was like Paolo Montero from the 90s, a man whose mere stare could make milk curdle, yet someone who was made even more special by a left foot that could distribute masterfully. Montero was not just brawn, he was also brains; two defenders rolled into one, steel draped in silk.

Latterly, the uncompromising Uruguayan captain Diego Lugano has taken that mantle for the national side. Shorn of pace, he makes up for this through leadership and a telegraphic reading of play. When Liverpool lost to his former side, Sao Paulo, in the Club World Championship

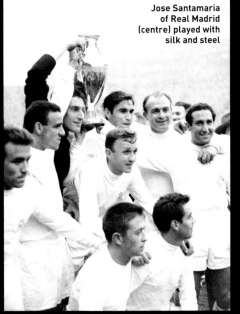

Jose Santamaria of Real Madrid (centre) played with silk and steel

Signed by Nacional at the age of 11, at 18 Coates was playing for their first-team. "The club has no other option but to produce its own players," he continues. "At the moment, Nacional relies on selling them on so the club can survive in the long-term. Over the last few years, Luis [Suarez] and Nicolas Lodeiro have been given a chance before being sold to European sides. (Lodeiro went for a then record £4m to Ajax). It's a sensible way to operate because everybody in Uruguay appreciates that the money invested in the league isn't there like it is in Brazil, Argentina or Europe.

"The club instills values into you that are important – how to conduct yourself on and off the pitch and how to appreciate what you have and treat people with respect. Without Nacional, I wouldn't be here now, I am certain of that."

> ## IN URUGUAY IT'S NACIONAL OR PENAROL, YOU EITHER FOLLOW ONE OR THE OTHER

of 2005, the corner count read 17-0 in favour of Liverpool. It seemed at times that Lugano was the only defender on the pitch for the Brazilians, his outstretched leg consistently just about intercepting the ball; there when you need him most.

As a teenager, Sebastian Coates grew up with posters of Montero, Lugano as well as former Argentine captain, Roberto Ayala, in his bedroom. The Liverpool centre-back, who like Luis Suarez, emerged from the Nacional team before landing in Europe says that the Montevideo club's youth system is the best in the country for producing young talent, especially in defensive areas.

"In Uruguay it's Nacional or Penarol," he says. "You either follow one or the other. My family were Nacional. It's a club that gives youth a chance. Luis is a striker but he can play anywhere – Nacional encourages that freedom. But if you are a defender like me, they want

you to think only about not conceding goals."

Coates admits that the influence of Suarez was crucial in his decision to move to Anfield.

"He helped me from a professional point of view. I knew about the history; the success and the European Cups, but he also taught me about the nature of the supporters – the way they treat the players. To be wanted by a club that is famous worldwide – by a club with a history like this, it was impossible to go anywhere else."

Suarez's own adaption to English football, too, was inspirational.

"Strikers are judged on their goals and if they move to a new club and start scoring early on, it makes life a lot easier. Football is like this; usually if you enjoy playing, your life off the pitch becomes easier. Luis' character, though, meant he was always going to settle quickly. He's a really passionate footballer – he plays each game like it's his last and is one of the most selfless players I've ever shared a dressing room with.

"Off the pitch, he is a very sociable person and this helps when you are moving to a new place."

7 GREAT SUAREZ GOALS

STOPPING LUIS SUAREZ IS ALMOST IMPOSSIBLE BECAUSE
THE TYPES OF GOALS HE SCORES ARE SO VARIED.
TAKING EXTRACTS FROM LFC MAGAZINE MATCH REPORTS,
HERE ARE SEVEN SUAREZ STRIKES TO SAVOUR

V FULHAM (W 5-2)
May 9, 2011

What LFC magazine said...

75mins JONJO Shelvey's pass sends Luis
Suarez clean through on goal and he skips
past the advancing Mark Schwarzer before
side-footing the ball into the next despite being
off balance. It's a sublime goal and one the
dynamic Uruguayan so richly deserves.

V SUNDERLAND (W 2-0)
March 20, 2011

What LFC magazine said...

77mins A MOMENT of inspiration from Liverpool's current number seven resulted in a beaming smile from their greatest one. Receiving a throw-in from the right flank, Suarez took a return pass and dribbled down the by-line, holding off a challenge from Lee Cattermole. Most people in the ground expected a pull-back or a floated cross, including goalkeeper Simon Mignolet. Instead, Suarez put his laces through the ball to make a mockery of the acute angle and score.

V WOLVES (W 2-1)
September 24, 2011

What LFC magazine said...

38mins SUAREZ sprang the Wolves offside trap to receive a fine throughball from Jose Enrique in the inside left channel. He then twisted and turned his way past Christophe Berra before hitting a low left-footed drive beyond Wayne Hennessey for a fantastic second at the Anfield Road end.

V ARSENAL (W 2-0)
August 20, 2011

What LFC magazine said...

90mins LUIS Suarez used his strength to turn Miquel on the touchline as he received Martin Kelly's chipped pass and slipped the ball to Lucas. The Brazilian drove forward and found Raul Meireles who slid a first-time pass back across the penalty area to Suarez. Goal. Game over.

V EVERTON (W 2-0)
October 1, 2011

What LFC magazine said...

82mins JAMIE Carragher's forward pass was nodded into Suarez's path by Dirk Kuyt and he drove into the box, taking on Leighton Baines and Sylvain Distin. The Everton pair seemed to have snubbed out the danger but ended up in a mess as Distin's clearance struck Suarez, who slid home his fifth of the season.

V NEWCASTLE (W 3-0)
May 1, 2011

What LFC magazine said...

65mins DIRK Kuyt played a part in the goal which made the game safe, teeing up Suarez to stroke home the third under pressure in front of the Kop.

V STOKE (W 2-1)
October 26, 2011

What LFC magazine said...

54 mins SUAREZ struck when Liverpool needed inspiring most. Shortly after the break he sprung his special move – the nutmeg; this one on Ryan Shotton, before curling with such grace beyond Thomas Sorensen that even some Stoke supporters clapped the finish.

What they said about him...

"We're delighted. He's got a fantastic goalscoring record. He's played in the World Cup and scored goals, he's played for Ajax and scored goals. I think he'll really excite the fans and it's great credit to the new owners, John and Tom, who've put a stamp down by bringing him here.

"All round it's a fantastic day for Liverpool Football Club. Luis scores goals. He's quick, he's intelligent, he's had a fantastic education at Ajax and we're looking forward to working with him and seeing him. Fingers crossed everybody will be happy."

KENNY DALGLISH On signing Suarez in January 2011

"Luis is going to bring the place alive because he is a street fighter. He arrived here with a decent reputation but he was not a big player then. In the dressing room he soon stood up and became a leader. That's why he was special.

"When he goes on his travels to South America he always rushes back.

"Suarez is back on the training pitch the next morning when he has just flown around half the world for a game for Uruguay. He immediately puts his focus on his club again.

"We'll remember him for his incredible amount of goals and what he has done for the club. Our fans were crazy about him."

RIK VAN DEN BOOG

Ajax managing director on why Suarez's hunger for success would make him a huge hit at Anfield

"Luis was fantastic. It is difficult sometimes to make your debut in a tight game but he came on and he quickly settled in.

"For him to come on and get a goal was brilliant and we are all delighted for him. It's definitely his goal. The law says if the ball is going on target it's your goal so he will take that."

GLEN JOHNSON

On Suarez's dream debut against Stoke City

"I'm sure that he will enjoy football in England and that he'll do very, very well. Of course if you compare the two leagues (England and Holland) it's totally different.

"But what I do believe and I always say from knowing first hand is if you get a Uruguayan player in your team, because of our mentality, you will always, always get something from him.

"Luis is a powerful player. He scores different goals, he can play up front on his own going everywhere or off a big striker like Carroll. Definitely I like him more when you play him up front. He can play in a two up front.

"He's very clever in his movements and of course he wants to get the ball in the position to score because he's a striker."

GUS POYET

On Suarez's potential to be a star in English football

"He speaks Dutch, which is good. Sometimes it is helpful to speak in the same language because defenders can't understand what you are saying.

"The times we have played together so far, I thought it went well. It will only get better and better. How excited was I when he signed? The first thing I told the lads and everyone around the club was that we had signed a top, top player.

"He is going to be very good for us. I'm sure of that. I phoned Luis just before the deal was completed and told him he was signing for a big club.

"He is adapting to things very quickly. He had to sort out a lot of things in his first week but every day in training he has been totally focused. He wants to be an important player for this club. He has shown already that he will be."

DIRK KUYT

On the prospect of a 'double Dutch' link-up in the Reds attack

"Already we can see what a good player Luis is. He's got good pace and awareness and he's settled in very quickly. He's a fighter too and the type of character he is means he's going to work really hard for the team.

"We've all been delighted with his first few performances. Hopefully there is even more to come from him too.

"I expect him to be even better when he adjusts to the speed of football in this country. He hadn't played many games in the weeks before he moved here so he's still getting his match fitness.

"When he gets that, he will be very difficult to stop."

STEVEN GERRARD

Speaking in February 2011

"I am about to pay Luis Suarez a major compliment - but after Sunday's performance he deserves it.

"The way the South American plays the game reminds me of the first time I saw Kevin Keegan in a Red shirt during the 1970s. Suarez is a breath of fresh air and he is just so infectious as he proved magnificently against Manchester United.

"He reminds me of Keegan with his balance and pace but also has elements of Kenny Dalglish in the way he backs into defenders using his backside.

"To think a player can show elements of those two legends of our club is incredibly exciting. He has settled into English football very quickly, which is not usually the case.

"The Uruguayan's energy ran throughout the team, he was tremendous and they could not handle him."

JOHN ALDRIDGE

After Suarez's destruction of Manchester United in March 2011

"Luis Suarez is an Anfield No.7 legend in the making.

"Forget about Fernando Torres taking time to adjust after a big move. Suarez has made it look easy since arriving from Ajax.

"He reminds me of Carlos Tevez; he's a real pocket rocket who plays with a big smile on his face.

"I think he'll prove to be a great acquisition for the Barclays Premier League, not just Liverpool."

JAMIE REDKNAPP

In March 2011

THE BIG MOVE TO EUROPE

In the second instalment of our look back at the career of Luis Suarez we speak to key figures at Dutch club Groningen to find out how the special striker achieved legendary status in just one season with his first European club

FINDING SUAREZ

"WE watched him for just 10 or 15 minutes and quickly knew he was a special player, that he could be great," Groningen technical manager Henk Veldmate vividly recalls.

"He was dribbling and showing special skills. The defenders were forced to foul him almost every time he got the ball. He was outstanding, particularly when you remembered he was only 19. He knew the way to the goal and knew exactly what to do to be decisive in a game."

That opinion was quickly formed five years ago. The player in action is now Liverpool's number seven and he had obviously impressed the watching Groningen contingent of Veldmate and managing director Hans Nijland.

They had made the 11,000-mile trek from northern Holland to South America in the hope of finding some new players, although Suarez wasn't the individual they had specifically travelled all that way to see.

"We actually went there to watch a central defender that weekend," Veldmate laughs. "But that didn't happen. Our contact in South America had also mentioned a guy named Luis Suarez. So we had heard the name but didn't know anything about him. That Saturday we watched him play for Nacional. Afterwards we asked his agent if it would be possible to speak with Luis."

Their scouting mission wasn't finished yet. With Suarez's performance still fresh in their minds they went to another game the following afternoon. A striker called Elias Ricardo Figueroa, a Uruguayan U17 and U20 international who played for Liverpool Montevideo, was the next player they analysed.

With plenty to think about, meetings between the Groningen officials and the players were arranged.

"Initially we didn't want to discuss anything financial with their agents," Veldmate says. "We wanted to learn about the individuals, find out if they were willing to move to Europe and what their family situation was. It was basically learning as much as we could about them and telling them about us. We thought it was important in helping us to make a decision."

After some debate it was agreed that Suarez was the preferred option.

"He was so confident, despite being so young.

>> "After speaking to him we thought he would have no problems coming to Holland. We felt he could go anywhere and flourish. We already had a Uruguayan player, central defender Bruno Silva, so we were sure that would help Luis too."

There was still one obstacle to completing the deal; the price. Nacional wanted more money for the Salto-born striker than Groningen had budgeted for.

"I'm not sure of the exact figure because it is a long time ago but I think we paid around 1.5m Euros in the end," Veldmate says. "For us that was a lot of money. We had never paid so much for a player before."

Breaking the club record fee for an unheard of Uruguayan striker was obviously a big risk. But, as Veldmate explains, it was one they felt they had to take.

"We were so convinced by his personality and his playing qualities we were sure it was a good decision. We thought he could help to take Groningen forward."

A SPECIAL PLAYER AND PERSON

THAT same summer FC Groningen also had another representative in Uruguay, albeit it in an unofficial capacity. Supporter Arnold Bloem was in South America to visit a friend and spend some time travelling.

Like all modern day fans he availed of the Internet to keep informed of happenings back at the Euroborg Stadium in Holland.

On a forum he read about a rumour suggesting the club were attempting to sign a Uruguayan striker. Then he learned a newspaper in Montevideo had mentioned a player named Luis Suarez could be joining Groningen. This potential signing was playing that very evening at the Luiz

>> Franzini-Stadium in the Uruguayan capital.

Naturally Bloem and the friend he had been visiting, Andre Das, made their way to the Nacional vs Central Espanol encounter. During the 1-1 draw he was impressed with the performance of the man his club were said to be interested in.

Afterwards, more in hope than expectation, they waited near the players' entrance to the stadium. When Suarez emerged the Spanish-speaking Das approached him.

"Suarez was friendly and said that he hoped and expected to join Groningen," Bloem remembers. "He told us he had spoken to Hans Nijland and Henk Veldmate and had also asked Bruno Silva about the club. He was enthusiastic about it. Then he left to go home – not by car or bicycle, but on foot!"

Bloem posted the story of his 'exclusive' chat on a Groningen forum. The next day the club confirmed they were in negotiations.

Two weeks later Bloem's adventure in Latin America concluded and he returned to Holland with a Uruguayan flag as a souvenir. By then Suarez was officially a Groningen player.

A NEW LIFE IN GRONINGEN

TWINNED with Newcastle, the town of Groningen in the north-east corner of Holland is situated close to the German border and nicknamed 'the City of Talent'.

A fifth of its 186,000 population are students, with the university having been in existence since 1614.

In contrast FC Groningen in its current form is only 40 years old, with its predecessor GVAV (Groningen Football and Athletic Union) having been established in 1915.

Some recognisable names to have worn the green and white shirt over the last four decades include Ronald and Erwin Koeman, Johan Neeskens and Arjen Robben.

In 1990/91 the club enjoyed probably their best season when they finished third in the top flight. However, that same decade also brought

relegation, before a return to the Eredivisie at the turn of the century.

Since 2005 they haven't finished outside the top eight, and in the middle of the 2005/06 campaign they swapped their old Oosterpark Stadium home for the brand new, 22,500-capacity, Euroborg Stadium.

Suarez was signed six months after that move to the intimate ground. If the boy who had spent his life living in first Salto, and then Montevideo, was curious about his new surroundings, the locals were also keen to learn about their latest arrival.

"Nobody knew anything," Jan Mennega, a reporter with Dagblad van het Noorden newspaper admits. "The only information we had was that he was young, from Uruguay and cost a lot of money.

"Naturally there were doubts about spending that amount on a player, especially someone unproven. I'm pretty sure that if Hans Nijland hadn't gone on the trip to Uruguay with Henk Veldmate then Suarez wouldn't have been signed. The fact that the director of football knew how good the player was too made a big difference. If Veldmate had just phoned up saying he wanted to spend that much on a player the answer probably would have been no.

"Word from the club was that he was amazing and would go on to be one of the best in Holland. Of course when the fans heard that they were even more eager to see him.

"At the press conference to unveil Suarez he didn't say much because he obviously couldn't speak the language. Despite that it was clear that the boy had an air of self confidence. He always looked people directly in the eye."

That inner strength was something the new arrival was going to need during his early days in Europe. Naturally Groningen was very different to where he had grown up, and acclimatising to those new surroundings took some time.

South African striker Glen Salmon and (former Fulham player) Erik Nevland were the side's chosen front pairing, meaning Suarez had to settle for a place on the bench when the team began the 2006/07 campaign with a home game against Feyenoord. He featured in the last four minutes of the 3-0 victory.

Some involvement with the reserve side provided a further taste of Dutch football until another outing in the first-team three weeks later, a UEFA Cup tie with FK Partizan Belgrade. The 4-2 away defeat meant progress to the next round was unlikely, but Suarez came off the bench for the final 18 minutes and managed to score.

"At the beginning it was not easy at all," Suarez said when reflecting upon those early days of life on a new continent.

"At that time I was not able to speak Dutch or English and communicating was incredibly hard. To add to this I needed some time to adjust to the Dutch league and I had to play with the second team of Groningen.

"What I always had clear in my mind was that I was not going to give up and that I would soon enough have an opportunity to prove myself."

> " **SUAREZ WAS FRIENDLY AND SAID THAT HE HOPED AND EXPECTED TO JOIN GRONINGEN. THEN HE LEFT TO GO HOME – NOT BY CAR OR BICYCLE, BUT ON FOOT!**

>>

THE 'UMBRELLA MATCH' AND THE 'MIRACULOUS MATCH'

THE most important man Suarez had to impress was Groningen coach Ron Jans, who had been in charge since October 2002.

The former striker wasn't on the scouting trip that had brought this unheard-of 19-year-old addition to his squad.

Instead he had remained in Holland and listened carefully to the views of Veldmate and Nijlands over the phone.

"I told them that if Hans Nijland alone had decided on this player I couldn't agree to the deal because he is a very impulsive man. But the fact that Henk also thought Suarez was special convinced me. I told them we had to go for it," Jans, who is now in charge of Heerenveen, says.

Like everyone else he eagerly awaited the first glimpse of the South American. Before that was possible though Suarez was allowed to go on holiday for three weeks as he had only recently stopped playing with Nacional. When he arrived in northern Holland, Jans immediately knew the club had found a good player.

"We didn't usually look in South America. From the first day you could see he was talented. He just needed to work on his fitness and his language skills. Despite this it was clear he was a good striker.

"We knew it would take him some time to get used to another country, another language and another way of playing."

Communication was the biggest issue of all. Jans' Spanish was limited so the services of Brazilian midfielder Hugo Alves Velame were called upon. He acted as a translator and slowly Suarez began to settle in.

On the first day of October everything changed for the better. Vitesse were the visitors to the Euroborg for a league game which Suarez would later refer to as 'the miraculous match.'

Despite playing well the home team found themselves 3-1 down with 10 minutes remaining. During a frantic finish Suarez earned a penalty,

Luis carries an umbrella – a symbol that he and his coach had settled their differences

which Koen van de Laak converted to halve the arrears.

Then, in the 89th and 91st minute, Suarez scored to provide a stunning 4-3 triumph. Amongst the jubilant scenes after the final whistle Jans handed the matchwinner an umbrella.

"It was a special day and a special moment," the manager recalls with a chuckle. "In the previous match I had taken Luis off because he wasn't fully fit. When he was coming off the pitch he was unhappy and showed it. That made me angry.

"It had been raining heavily and there was an umbrella near me. I threw it in Luis' direction. Afterwards we had a good conversation and worked things out.

"When the Vitesse game finished I gave him the umbrella to prove that everything was good between us again. When he and the team were celebrating he showed it to the crowd. It's a good memory for me and I'm sure it is for him too.

"Early on it was a bit of a struggle with Luis but we got there in the end. He stole my heart."

Jans' emotional words were backed up by his team selections. Following that afternoon Suarez was a regular starter in the side for the remainder of the season.

LUIS' PARTING GIFT

WITH Suarez and Erik Nevland now the recognised strike force, goals were always likely. The problem they had was that keeping a clean sheet was a rare occurrence.

Groningen's next outing after the drama of Vitesse illustrated this perfectly. Twice they netted in the Amsterdam Arena – Suarez scoring the first – but a narrow 3-2 reversal ensued.

In just over a month Heerenveen put four past them. The low point of the season saw FC Twente register seven and ADO Den Haag left the Euroborg with a 5-2 win. Amongst all that there was also a cup exit against NAC Breda.

Renewing acquaintances with Vitesse seemed to bring the best out of Suarez. Again he netted a brace, although this time it was during a 3-2 defeat. That was in mid-January.

With a dozen games remaining Jans knew

Ron Jans was Suarez's coach at Groningen

HE ALWAYS LEARNS QUICKLY, HE IS A VERY INTELLIGENT FOOTBALLER

his side needed to produce the consistency that had eluded them if they were to reach the play-offs for the UEFA Cup places.

They did it by embarking on a run of just two defeats in their final 12 fixtures, with seven victories in that sequence.

By this point Suarez had netted a dozen times in all competitions, although some reporters were claiming that he was too selfish.

Jans quickly refutes those arguments. "People said he was playing for himself. But when you looked at the stats he had provided the most assists too so it wasn't true. Luis and Nevland needed to get to know each other. When they did they formed a really good partnership."

Feyenoord were the first side standing in Groningen's way in the play-offs. A 2-1 home win followed by a 1-1 away draw moved Suarez and his colleagues closer to the coveted prize.

Utrecht, who had overcome Roda JC on away goals, were their opponents in the final.

Prior to the two-legged affair Suarez illustrated his sense of humour by asking Nevland when he was going to create a goal for him.

Naturally Nevland did provide an assist, as Suarez scored twice in the first leg to provide a 2-0 victory.

He followed it up with the opener in the second leg as Groningen went on to record an emphatic 4-1 aggregate win and secure European qualification for 2007/08.

The gamble of bringing in an unknown teenager had paid off in a huge way. When asked to sum up Suarez's impact, an enthusiastic Jans says: "He became one of our most important players. That's a very big achievement when you are 19, and have arrived from a country where the climate, the culture, the language, the people, the food - everything - are totally different. You have to be really special to adapt so quickly at such a young age.

"He always learns quickly, he is a very intelligent footballer. Every season he seems to get better and better and I think he will continue to do so at Liverpool."

Arnold Bloem, the fan who had met Suarez in Uruguay the previous summer, was in attendance for the win over Utrecht and had his Uruguayan flag with him. Suarez spotted it and wrapped himself in it as the players did a lap of honour.

Before the jubilant crowd and squad

eventually went their separate ways the forward returned the flag to its owner. Some blood from a cut on Suarez's knee had made its way onto the blue and white stripes and is still there now. Bloem hopes his extra special South American souvenir will one day end up in the club museum.

Suarez only had a solitary season with Groningen, yet his performances and goals haven't been forgotten. With the club celebrating its 40th anniversary in 2011 Dag Blad van het Noorden newspaper ran a readers' poll to select FCG's best ever side. Our current number seven was chosen as one of the forwards.

WHAT DID YOU THINK WHEN LIVERPOOL INITIALLY SHOWED THEIR INTEREST IN YOU?

"When Liverpool first contacted Ajax, I wanted to give the club a chance to present itself to me and my family first then allow us to gain our own impressions. I could have spoken to someone like Diego Forlan (the former Manchester United striker) who has played at Anfield and experienced the Premier League before. But in life you need to make your own opinion so I spoke to Liverpool with an open mind - even though I was immediately excited about their interest."

SUAREZ SIGNS IN...

REDS GO UNDER THE RADAR TO BRING IN A WORLD CLASS TALENT THE GAME'S BIGGEST CLUBS WOULD HAVE WANTED

WHEN Kenny Dalglish returned as manager eight days into January, the Reds' director of football Damien Comolli had already been plotting a move for Luis Suarez. And when Dalglish confirmed his interest in increasing his attacking options by adding the talented Uruguayan, the Reds pushed on with those plans.

The club's scouting team had long been convinced of Suarez's attributes but the player was also courted by others and doubts remained over whether Ajax would let him leave and the size of fee they would demand.

For a fortnight newspaper speculation about a possible deal was rife, though many sources suggested a difference in the clubs' valuation of the player could see the move break down.

On the morning of January 28, Ajax coach Frank de Boer was reported in the Dutch media as saying he felt there was a '50-50 chance' that the deal would go through.

Later that day, LFC issued the following statement: 'Liverpool Football Club announced this afternoon that they had agreed a fee of up to 26.5million Euros with Ajax for the transfer of Luis Suarez, subject to the completion of a medical.'

Fans were excited by Fenway Sports Group's imminent investment and the prospect of seeing Suarez link up with Fernando Torres.

However, Suarez's arrival soon took on extra significance as Torres rocked the club with a transfer request and subsequently left for Chelsea in a £50 million transfer.

A new number nine, Andy Carroll, followed Suarez into the club and suddenly Kopites had the prospect of seeing a new-look strike force in action.

Talking to LFC magazine, Comolli explained why the club had made the signings.

He said: "We didn't have a lot of time (to prepare for the January window) and that's why we went for players who we knew very well such as Andy and Luis. You can go into a window as prepared as you think you possibly can be and then something will trigger events that you didn't expect. That's why I always tell scouts that they have to be prepared for every possible scenario we can think of. We have to be ready as a scouting staff to come up with ideas and solutions. Sometimes those ideas are of use, sometimes they are not. But the good thing about what happened in January was that we were very comfortable with the two players because we knew them very well.

"In Andy's case, he was based in England so we knew a lot about him and with Luis we knew what he had done during the last three or four years playing in Europe and also what he did at the World Cup.

"I think that's where intelligence on the ground becomes very, very important because we never thought Luis would be available in January. I don't think many people knew he would be available in January and certainly not at the price that we paid when you consider that after the World Cup Ajax wanted double that amount. So there was an opportunity and we kept it very quiet. I think one of the reasons we managed to do the deal was because we kept it under the radar.

"Very often the press will ask why we don't make things more public. Well the obvious answer regarding the Luis deal - and even with Andy - is that if anything had come out, maybe a lot of other clubs would have come in for the player. Because we were the only ones to know, we were first and able to do the deals."

KENNY ON SUAREZ
"I think everyone has their own identity and it undermines the boy if you compare him with anyone else. He is Luis Suarez. He is a fantastic player and it is not fair to compare him with others who have been here before.

"Does he benefit from working with me? I don't know - I don't speak Espanol! I don't know where he gets his ideas from but he is full of them and he certainly knows how to play.

"The fans take to him because he is so genuine and 100 per cent committed. The crowd love players like that. He is just a fantastic player."

- On why the fans love our number seven

SUAREZ ON KENNY
"He [Dalglish] is a person who you respect after only a few minutes conversation. He tried to speak to me in Spanish – 'hola, bienvenido' (hello and welcome) – the basics and that impressed me. Obviously, he is a legend at this club...in this city, but I think it's very important to judge people as you see them rather than just what you hear. He has lived up to that legend in my eyes."

- On living up to the legend

SUAREZ ON KENNY
"I could see quickly that Dalglish is a manager and a person who I can relate to and he is very determined to make the team play with a certain image – the kind of attractive football that I want to be a part of. He was very keen to bring me here and if there is one person that was influential in my signing it was him. He is very ambitious about the club and is confident he can lead the club back to the top. Now I am here, I do not want to disappoint him in any way."

- On spearheading a team that plays good football

SUAREZ ON KENNY
"It's getting better. He does try to say a few words to me in Spanish and that's a good sign. I'm trying to say a few words in English too."

- On Kenny's Spanish

MUTUAL RESPECT

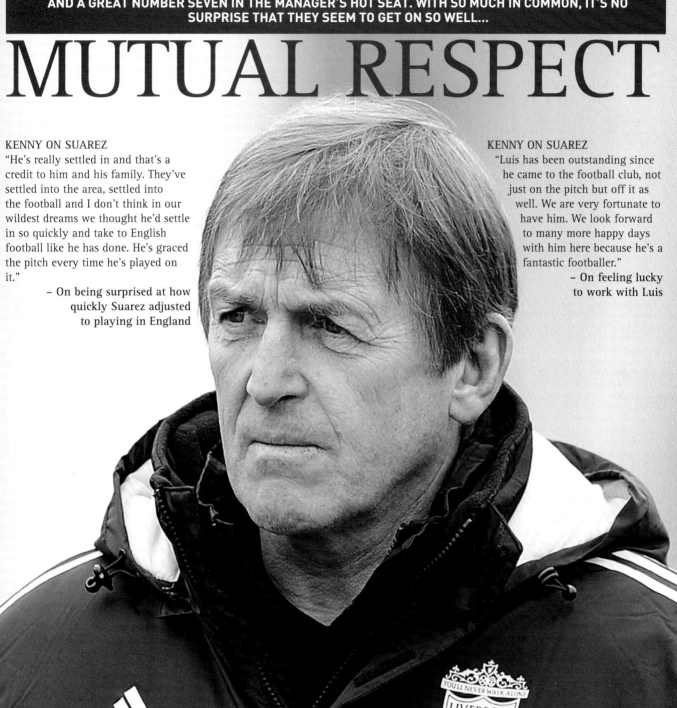

KENNY ON SUAREZ

"He's really settled in and that's a credit to him and his family. They've settled into the area, settled into the football and I don't think in our wildest dreams we thought he'd settle in so quickly and take to English football like he has done. He's graced the pitch every time he's played on it."

– On being surprised at how quickly Suarez adjusted to playing in England

KENNY ON SUAREZ

"Luis has been outstanding since he came to the football club, not just on the pitch but off it as well. We are very fortunate to have him. We look forward to many more happy days with him here because he's a fantastic footballer."

– On feeling lucky to work with Luis

"I hadn't realised its history when I asked for the number seven. I was asked what number and I chose it. But now I'm quite happy that I did, now I know about players like Kenny Dalglish and Kevin Keegan. I have seen some videos of Dalglish scoring for Liverpool. He was a great player. But the number I've got on the back of my shirt is the last thing on my mind when I go out to play. I just go out to try and do my best. It certainly doesn't add any weight of expectation more than any other number would do for me"

Luis Suarez, 2011

Wearing the number 7

ALTHOUGH there were experiments in earlier years, notably the 1933 FA Cup final when Everton wore 1-11 and Manchester City wore 12-22, it was July 5, 1939 before the Football League management committee sanctioned the use of shirt numbers.

So, on August 26, 1939, South African winger Berry Nieuwenhuys became the first player to officially wear the now-famous number seven shirt for Liverpool FC in a 2-1 defeat against Sheffield United at Bramall Lane. Less than a week later, World War II broke out. When the Football League resumed in 1946 it was 'Nivvy' who again wore the number seven shirt, this time in a 1-0 win over the Blades at Bramall Lane.

Since then, 17 players have worn Liverpool's number seven on what could be considered a regular basis, while many others have appeared in it occasionally.

Kevin Keegan and Kenny Dalglish gave the shirt its legendary status at Anfield in the 1970s and 1980s, but they aren't the only ones to have enjoyed success with it on their backs.

The introduction of squad numbers in 1993/94, the Premier League's second year, means that just six men have worn the Liverpool number seven shirt during the last 19 seasons.

Luis Suarez is now the man in possession. He's in some illustrious company.

LIVERPOOL NUMBER 7s – 1939 TO 2011

BERRY NIEUWENHUYS
JIMMY PAYNE
BRIAN JACKSON
BILLY LIDDELL
FRED MORRIS
KEVIN LEWIS
IAN CALLAGHAN
KEVIN KEEGAN
KENNY DALGLISH
PAUL WALSH
PETER BEARDSLEY
DEAN SAUNDERS
NIGEL CLOUGH
STEVE McMANAMAN
VLADIMIR SMICER
HARRY KEWELL
ROBBIE KEANE
LUIS SUAREZ

QQLS...

DOES THE LARGE TRANSFER FEE THE CLUB PAID OUT PUT PRESSURE ON YOU?

"I am aware that the fee Liverpool paid for me was big, but I'm not going to worry about that. There will be a pressure from the outside for me to succeed but every time I set foot on to a football pitch, I want to enjoy it. Some players can become obsessed with the pressure and trying to deal with it, but I think it is important to be yourself - try your best and believe in yourself."

ON HIS NEVER
SAY DIE ATTITUDE

V MANCHESTER UNITED
15.10.2011

"Something that I learnt from a very young age early on in my football career was that you never give up. You never give up on a ball as a lost cause, you fight for everything...you never drop your head for one minute and you keep trying until the last whistle. And if you know that skill-wise or technique-wise it's not your day and things aren't quite coming off for you, it just means that you try even harder... you close people down and you press and you get tackles in. I think it's important to have that spirit and that never say die attitude."

What they said about him...

"Luis is a great player and I'm really looking forward to building a successful partnership with him. You can see what he's all about and the range of skills that he has.

"I feel that we've been working really well together in training and the partnership's going from strength to strength."

ANDY CARROLL

On his strike partnership with Suarez, speaking in April 2011

"It's always difficult, especially for the foreign boys coming in, to make such a big impact. If I had to pick one who made a similar impact it would maybe be Gianfranco Zola.

"I was at Chelsea at the time he came in, and I think in his first season he only played for seven months but got the Football Writers' Player of the Year award, which tells you he made a big impact.

"I see similar things in Luis, which is fantastic. Luis' style and the way he plays is what has helped him.

"He likes to be involved in the action all of the time, he's not afraid of the physical stuff, he likes to be in and about and get on the ball, and I think you've seen inside the penalty box he is a danger to anybody."

STEVE CLARKE

On the impact Suarez had during his first few months at the club

"The groundwork and intelligence coming out from the scouting team was very good. Everything you look at with Luis - his character, his attitude, his commitment, on top of all the football skills - made us feel he was the right person and the right individual. He had opportunities to join other clubs, including in the Premier League, during the window, but as soon as we started talking to him he was very committed and was saying: 'I only want to play for Liverpool, I only want to come to Liverpool'. The more the player gives you this feedback then the more you are inclined to do the maximum to get him. It's an extra motivation.

"He was saying: 'Please come and get me, I want to play for Liverpool'. The more he was saying that the more motivated we were to get him. Since he arrived he has shown his talent and everything else from the personality point of view."

DAMIEN COMOLLI

Reds' director of football on the qualities that attracted the club to Suarez

"Everybody has been talking about how good he is. I think you could see why he is at this club. He's a top player and he took his goal well.

"It was nice to get the assist but the important thing is the team winning. We are disappointed with a draw. It's not the best start but there are plenty of games to go."

CHARLIE ADAM

After the 1-1 draw with Sunderland in the opening game of the 2011/12 season

"If he [Suarez] keeps playing like that I think he'll be a bigger legend than I'll ever be. He looks a really top player, he plays for the team. It shows he's adaptable and versatile, he can do different jobs for the teams."

JAMIE CARRAGHER

On Suarez's sensational start in a red shirt

"I know he's only been at Liverpool four months but my player of the season is Luis Suarez.

"For me, Suarez has lit the place up. We were all in need of a lift at the end of January and he has provided it. Suarez has been magnificent and I've loved watching him."

JOHN ALDRIDGE

On his 2010/11 LFC Player of the Season

"I found it amazing he was allowed to play in Holland for as long as he did, with his goals record and what he's done internationally as well.

"I never had any doubts. He can play anywhere on the field, and by that I mean he pops up everywhere and is almost impossible to mark.

"He's a very comfortable two-footed player, he sees a pass, he can dribble. I always say to people: that's what a good player looks like.

"We have a great, great player at this club and his job now is to go on and become one of the all-time greats at Anfield, and he's got all the tools to do that."

JAN MOLBY

On why Suarez will become a Liverpool legend

"Luis Suarez looks a fantastic player - I don't really know what else to add to that. I was a bit tentative when he first came because obviously his record in Holland was very good but there have been players who've come from Holland in the past and not set the Premier League alight.

"But I was happy with his performances straight away and he looks like he's going to be a very good player for Liverpool."

ROBBIE FOWLER On Luis getting off to a fast start

THE 'IRON MAN' OF AJAX

As the career of Luis Suarez really begins to take off, we speak to Dutch journalists and staff at Ajax to find out how the mercurial attacker made a huge impression with Holland's most famous club to pave the way for his Anfield move

ARRIVING AT AJAX

RAFA BENITEZ'S purchase of Ryan Babel for Liverpool in the summer of 2007 meant the Dutch side needed to add another attacking option to their squad.

With Luis Suarez scoring against them both home and away during the previous season he had obviously troubled their defenders, and given the Amsterdam club a close-up glimpse of his capabilities.

Fifteen goals in 37 appearances for Groningen had helped them qualify for the UEFA Cup and alerted clubs to his potential. It was Ajax who moved first to acquire him.

"They didn't have to be geniuses to sign Suarez," Jop van Kempen of Het Parool newspaper in Amsterdam points out. "Henk Ten Cate (former Chelsea assistant manager) was in charge then. I would compare buying him to Manchester United buying Louis Saha a few years ago. Everyone could see he was a good player and it made sense to get him.

"It wasn't like when some clubs end up with really good players unexpectedly. PSV were always good at that. When they got Romario nobody knew who he was. All of a sudden he was there and he was brilliant. That was in the time before the Internet and you didn't see football from all over the world then.

"With Suarez all the credit for spotting him and bringing him to Europe goes to Groningen and their people. After that everyone could see how good he was. Buying him from them was an easy choice."

Completing the deal wasn't so simple though. Understandably Groningen were reluctant to let the impressive star depart the Euroborg Stadium after just a solitary campaign.

"They refused the first offer," van Kempen continues. "Suarez made it clear that he wanted to leave to better himself at a bigger club. The deal went to arbitration before the Dutch FA and dragged on for a long time. Eventually Ajax offered 8.5m Euros and it was accepted."

In early August, Suarez was confirmed as their player. Some people may have considered the price-tag high for a forward with just one season in European football.

Mike Verweij of De Telegraaf newspaper disagrees with such views. "No, definitely not," he says. "In Amsterdam the people still think that was the deal of the millennium. It was a great piece of business."

ADAPTING ALL OVER AGAIN

A RECORD of 111 goals in 159 games during three-and-a-half seasons reinforces the opinion that Suarez was a huge success in the city on the banks of the Amstel river.

Roberto De Cock from the Ajax supporters club lists him as amongst the club's most important players over the last decade, alongside names such as Rafael van der Vaart, Wesley Sneijder, Zlatan Ibrahimovich and Klaas-Jan Huntelaar.

Suarez showed he was a man of the people in Holland, taking a ride through town and performing a role reversal as he takes a photo of a fan

Ajax was the purr-fect move for Luis and the club mascot (right) certainly agrees, while Martin Jol put great faith in Suarez, and the fans, who he's signing autographs for, certainly appreciated him too

The Ajax fans (left) hold up a banner to thank Luis Suarez for his contribution to the club

SUAREZ BEDANKT

>>

At first though Suarez had to adapt to life at a new club all over again, just as he had done 12 months earlier with Groningen.

Huntelaar had been at Ajax since December 2005 and was already well established as the

"LUIS IS UNPREDICTABLE, HE'S HARD TO INFLUENCE BUT THAT MAKES HIM SPECIAL

main striker, and a prolific one too. (He would eventually finish his time at the club with 76 league goals). This meant the new signing usually operated on the left or the right of the attack.

There was also a different boss to work with and Suarez later described Ten Cate as "demanding and hard." Yet in the same sentence he also declared that the move was good for him. Playing with better players helped his game to improve, even if he needed some guidance initially.

"When he first arrived he was different to the Suarez Liverpool fans recognise," Van Kempen remembers. "He had long hair and usually played with his shirt outside his shorts. These things are not allowed at Ajax.

"Apparently his girlfriend and his Uruguay team-mate Diego Forlan encouraged him to change and to adapt to the mentality of a big club. I think they were a big influence."

Adjusting his mindset didn't appear to impact too much on his ability to play the same type of football he'd produced at Groningen.

This was despite Ten Cate leaving the club to join Chelsea that October and Adrie Koster taking over as interim coach.

Those alterations in the dugout apparently did little to affect the side who challenged PSV for the title. The 94 goals they scored were more than any of their rivals, with Suarez netting 17 of that total He also registered five more in other competitions. Yet it wasn't enough to overhaul Eindhoven who took the title by three points.

WORKING WITH VAN BASTEN
AFTER Holland were eliminated at the quarter-final of the 2008 European Championships, Marco van Basten became Ajax coach and Suarez continued to impress.

"Ron Jans, his boss at Groningen, had told me about how good Luis was and especially how good he was at going past defenders," Van Kempen says. "Dribbling is one of his main skills. The number of times he plays the ball against an opponent's legs and then runs on to it again is so frequent that it can't be accidental.

"He seems to have a very good sense of how defenders move and he is able to find their weak spots. When he works this out he attacks those weak sides. He did this at Ajax all the time."

Other aspects of his play which endeared him

to regulars at the Arena was his work rate and passion for the club.

"Luis is unpredictable, he's hard to influence but that makes him special," Van Basten said.

Van Basten was well aware of the forward's contribution to the side as he stated: "Suarez is extremely important to us. He is involved in almost all the goals that we score."

That December, Huntelaar, who had been linked with numerous clubs, joined Real Madrid in a deal worth close to 20m Euros. His absence didn't hinder Suarez's form, as he registered his best tally in a season by finishing with 28 goals.

That still wasn't enough to help the four-time European champions to their first Eredivise title since 2004. Instead AZ Alkmaar claimed the crown, with FC Twente occupying second spot and Van Basten's squad a further point adrift of them. Missing out on the Champions League led to a new manager taking charge.

Yet Suarez had learnt plenty from the man who scored THAT stunning volley in Euro '88. "He taught me a lot about how to play as a forward," the Uruguayan said of his departed boss, "about shooting techniques and about things that worked for him. His movement, his technique."

JOL TAKES OVER
MARTIN Jol took Van Basten's place, and his first major decision was to install Suarez as captain.

Naturally the player warmly welcomed this choice. "It was a surprise to me that he had made that decision but it made me feel very happy," Suarez admitted. "Martin made me a better player. He made me feel important."

This new responsibility was obviously something Suarez took seriously, and during his time as skipper he tried to help a clearly talented squad reach their full potential.

"Even now, a lot of the young players at the club still speak very highly of Luis," Verweij points out. "They say he always had time for them and he taught them a lot about playing the game and how to live like a footballer. He also taught them to win.

"In Holland a lot of young players play well, but don't help their teams to win. Over the last few years Ajax have had plenty of good players. But for a while success seemed to elude them.

Suarez's best game for Ajax?

JOP VAN KEMPEN (HAT PAROOL newspaper):

"It was probably against AC Milan in the Champions League in Amsterdam. He played very well against Nesta, I remember he nut-megged him a few times. That was definitely one of his best games, especially when you considered the level of the opponents."

"Suarez said the team had the right quality but needed the winning mentality to go with it. He had learned about that while growing up in Uruguay.

"Luis said they needed to develop that killer instinct if they were to be successful."

The skipper's example matched his words. He found the net 35 times in the league, in just 33 appearances. He also scored half-a-dozen in the UEFA Cup and another eight in the domestic cup. It meant he'd registered a stunning 49 goals from 48 games.

Agonisingly, it wasn't enough to deliver the championship. Instead Steve McClaren's FC Twente picked up the shield for the first time ever. This occurred despite Ajax producing a run of 14 straight wins at one stage. The final gap between the teams was just a solitary point.

Jol's squad did have the consolation of cup success, as they comprehensively defeated Feyenoord over two legs. A 2-0 triumph at home was followed by a 4-1 away victory just four days after missing out on the title. Suarez netted twice in the second game to conclude the season with celebrations.

The captain was also the recipient of personal silverware as he was named Dutch player of the year, after equalling Mateja Kezman's record of league goals by a foreigner. His overall impact was demonstrated by the fact he

Luis received a hero's reception (top right) when he went back to Ajax shortly after joining the Reds

led the way with assists too, creating 17 goals for his colleagues.

THE IRON MAN IMPRESSES

WATCHING Uruguay's games at the 2010 World Cup stirred mixed emotions for Ajax supporters. Rightly they were proud to see their own captain do so well.

Simultaneously, they realised his form the previous year plus his three goals in South Africa meant the chances of him leaving had multiplied.

"For Ajax fans that is a worry they carry with them 365 days of the year," Van Kempen explains. "Every summer they sell players. The Dutch league is a selling league and Ajax is a selling club. Prior to the World Cup Jol had joked: 'I hope Suarez does well, but not too well.' He knew if Luis performed at his best there was a chance other clubs would want him."

Apart from incoming bids, another concern for those with Ajax connections was what effect the summer exertions would have on their star player.

Starting a post-World Cup season below par is not uncommon. And giving players in that category a rest is often the suggested solution. Suarez didn't agree. He just wanted to continue playing. In the previous four seasons he had rarely missed a game through injury or tiredness, with only the odd suspension ever ruling him out. Journalists had noted this ability to play week in, week out, and quizzed him about what appeared to be immunity to injury.

"He told us that he had been injured on a few occasions but hadn't told the coach about it," Verweij recalls. "Some managers might not see that as the best idea but it's a great example of how much he wanted to play, even if he wasn't 100 per cent right.

"I think his pain threshold is very high. It was very unusual to ever hear him complain about being tired or unfit. Reporters would say he'd play on one leg if he could. People started

---

Suarez's best goal for Ajax?

MIKE VERWEIJ (DE TELEGRAAF newspaper):

"It is difficult to pick his best goal, because he scored lots of beautiful ones. His most important goal was against Dynamo Kiev in the Champions League qualifier. That was really important for the club to get through because they earned a lot of money from it. They needed that because Ajax are not rich.

When he first arrived all of his goals seemed to come from inside the area, or inside the six-yard box. They called him 'the new Pippo Inzaghi' because he scored only those kind of goals.

Eventually that changed though and he started to score lots of different types. When he left in January there was a video of his 20 best goals on the Internet. There could have been 50 because he scored so many great ones."

 ## HE BECAME TOO GOOD FOR OUR LEAGUE AND IS DOING WELL IN THE PREMIER LEAGUE

>> referring to him as 'the iron man.'"

His strong-willed nature was needed instantly. There was no time for rest after helping his country to fourth place in South Africa.

At the end of July, Ajax's Champions League campaign began with a qualifier against PAOK of Greece. Suarez scored in both legs as the tie finished 4-4 on aggregate and the Dutch team progressed on away goals.

The second half of August brought the third qualifying round, and the much tougher task of Dynamo Kiev. A 1-1 draw in Ukraine was followed by a 2-1 home win in Holland, with Suarez again getting on the scoresheet.

That hard work brought them a group consisting of Real Madrid, AC Milan and Auxerre. Disappointingly progression to the knockout stages wasn't achieved.

Exiting the Champions League prior to Christmas brought a premature end to Jol's tenure in early December. He was replaced by Frank de Boer.

The new man only worked with Suarez for a few weeks before the attacker became a Liverpool player. In that time De Boer

obviously saw enough to realise just how good he is.

"I rate him very highly," the former Dutch international said. "In the Netherlands he developed himself very well. He is always a threat for defenders, he is always busy.

"He became too good for our league and he is doing well in the Premier League. I would definitely put him in the top 20 attackers in Europe."

When he left Holland at the end of January a video of his best goals appeared on the Ajax website, entitled 'Adios Suarez'. The compilation contains some of his stunning efforts in red and white. It illustrated that, although he had departed, the club hadn't forgotten his efforts.

In February he returned to the Arena to bid the fans farewell and they serenaded him with a rendition of You'll Never Walk Alone.

Their warmth is something Suarez gladly returns. He once celebrated a goal by unveiling a t-shirt that consisted of two halves; one Uruguay and the other Ajax.

In his absence his team-mates also showed they still remembered him as they went on to become champions. They had developed the killer instinct at last.

He knows how to
Celebrate

ALMOST as exciting as Luis Suarez's goals and pieces of individual skill are his celebrations. As he explains in the exclusive interview at the front of this special edition, he never plans what he is going to do after a goal goes in. He simply reacts automatically. One thing that is for sure, he has given us many memorable post-goal moments is his Reds career so far. Here are some pictures of the best ones...

LUIS SUAREZ
QUIZ
& COMPETITION

SO you just can't get enough of Luis Suarez, but have you learnt everything about him? You can put your Luis knowledge to the test by taking our Suarez Quiz and if you know the answer to question number seven then you could be in with a chance of winning one of three copies of The Suarez Story that have been signed by Liverpool's number 7. **Good luck...**

1. From which club did Liverpool sign Luis Suarez?

2. Name the Uruguayan town where Luis Suarez was born.

3. What is Luis Suarez's nickname in Uruguay?

4. Against which nation did Luis Suarez score in the 2011 Copa America final?

5. Which club did Luis Suarez score against on his Carling Cup debut for Liverpool?

6. Who was the last player to wear our famous number 7 shirt before Luis Suarez?

7. Against which club did Luis Suarez score his first goal for Liverpool?

DAZZLING
DEBUT

"I think it is a dream debut. Anyone would say it is a dream debut. Just to be on the field for a few minutes and to manage to score in front of the Kop, it's what dreams are made of.
"I hope I can score as many *(goals as I did in Holland)*. The first target for me is to help the team whether it's scoring goals or just helping the team out in general play, because what counts is the team, not individuals"

THE January 2011 transfer window was Fenway Sports Group's first opportunity to show their intent in the transfer market.

And they demonstrated their backing when, after skilful negotiations between Damien Comolli and Ajax, the Reds broke their transfer record to sign coveted Uruguayan striker Luis Suarez.

However, the fanfare surrounding Suarez's £22.8 million move from the Dutch capital was a little drowned out by subsequent events on transfer deadline day.

Fernando Torres left the club for Chelsea in a £50 million switch while Andy Carroll joined the Reds from Newcastle for a reported £35 million as the club smashed their transfer record again.

Despite the sideshow of the Torres transfer, there was an air of expectation surrounding Suarez.

Pundits in Holland and South America were unanimous in their opinion that the Uruguay international could set the Premier League alight.

Liverpool's first fixture following his transfer was a home game against Stoke City on February 2.

However Suarez, who was handed the Reds' historic number seven shirt, had barely played in more than a month. And, in addition to a few concerns over his match fitness, there was also an amount of bureaucracy to be overcome before he could make his debut.

There was a fear that red tape would make him unavailable for the visit of the Potters as the club awaited international clearance and a work permit.

In the event, the paper work was completed in time for him to come into contention and Kenny Dalglish named his new forward on the substitutes' bench.

Liverpool were already a goal to the good when Dalglish gave Suarez the nod to warm up. And in the 63rd minute, he received a rapturous reception as he entered the Anfield turf for the first time, replacing Fabio Aurelio.

In his 27-minute cameo, he showed more than enough to suggest the Kop had a new idol in their midst.

His clever link-up play and movement was a feature of his first appearance in a red shirt.

And he needed just 16 minutes to crown his bow with a goal.

A clever flick by Dirk Kuyt sent Suarez through in front of the Kop.

He bore down on Stoke goalkeeper Asmir Begovic before rounding him and shooting towards goal. Backtracking Potters defender Andy Wilkinson did his utmost to keep Suarez's shot out but succeeded only in deflecting it into the net off the post.

The goal gave the Reds a 2-0 win - their third consecutive victory - and left supporters eagerly anticipating their next glimpse of Suarez in the Liverpool attack.

What they said about him...

"He's still young enough and I'm sure he's going to get even better than he is now, which is a scary thought.

"He's got the appetite for the game to learn and get better. Hopefully he will go on here for a long time because he's certainly got a massive part to play at this club in the future - the history is there to be written."

STEVEN GERRARD
On why Suarez can join Liverpool's greats

"Sometimes you think you are signing a great player and you have different opinions about them.

"But it is only when you train with them every day that you know their strengths and weaknesses. I know there are great players in the league; Aguero has started well, so has Rooney, but I can honestly say I wouldn't swap him for anyone. I think he is fantastic."

JAMIE CARRAGHER
On why he wouldn't swap Suarez

"For me, he has to be the best signing any club has made in the last 12 months.

"No matter who the opposition is, he always has an influence on the game. He's a brilliant player and I've lost count of the number of times I've heard supporters from other clubs saying 'I wish we'd signed him.'

"Liverpool are so lucky to have him because in my opinion he's going to become - if he isn't already - an international superstar."

ALAN HANSEN
On why Suarez is the signing of 2011

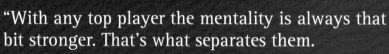

"With any top player the mentality is always that bit stronger. That's what separates them.
"There are a lot of good players at this level and the really, really top ones have got that mental edge that drives them on all the time and produces the kind of performances that we've had from Luis so far. He's very grounded.
"He comes back in on Monday morning and works as hard as ever in training, he upsets all the defenders, scores a couple of goals and that's what he's all about.
"He trains like he plays - absolutely, every day. He loves to be playing football and that's a great thing."

STEVE CLARKE September 2011

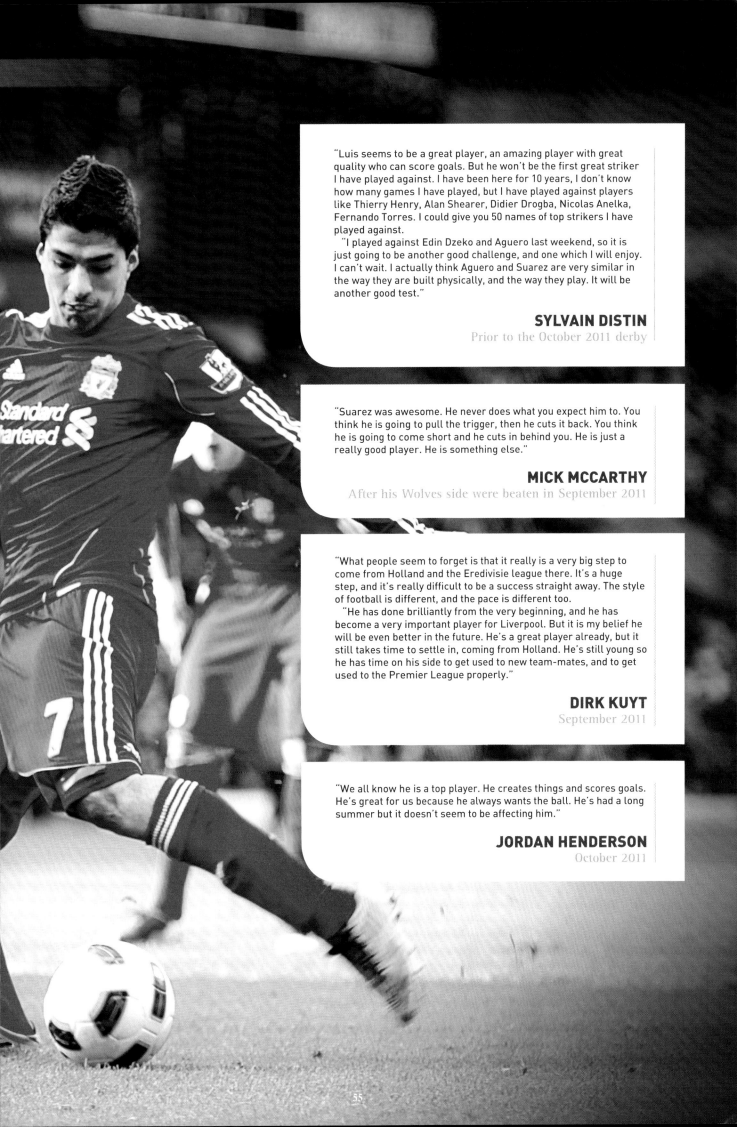

"Luis seems to be a great player, an amazing player with great quality who can score goals. But he won't be the first great striker I have played against. I have been here for 10 years, I don't know how many games I have played, but I have played against players like Thierry Henry, Alan Shearer, Didier Drogba, Nicolas Anelka, Fernando Torres. I could give you 50 names of top strikers I have played against.

"I played against Edin Dzeko and Aguero last weekend, so it is just going to be another good challenge, and one which I will enjoy. I can't wait. I actually think Aguero and Suarez are very similar in the way they are built physically, and the way they play. It will be another good test."

SYLVAIN DISTIN
Prior to the October 2011 derby

"Suarez was awesome. He never does what you expect him to. You think he is going to pull the trigger, then he cuts it back. You think he is going to come short and he cuts in behind you. He is just a really good player. He is something else."

MICK MCCARTHY
After his Wolves side were beaten in September 2011

"What people seem to forget is that it really is a very big step to come from Holland and the Eredivisie league there. It's a huge step, and it's really difficult to be a success straight away. The style of football is different, and the pace is different too.

"He has done brilliantly from the very beginning, and he has become a very important player for Liverpool. But it is my belief he will be even better in the future. He's a great player already, but it still takes time to settle in, coming from Holland. He's still young so he has time on his side to get used to new team-mates, and to get used to the Premier League properly."

DIRK KUYT
September 2011

"We all know he is a top player. He creates things and scores goals. He's great for us because he always wants the ball. He's had a long summer but it doesn't seem to be affecting him."

JORDAN HENDERSON
October 2011

NATIONAL HERO

Continuing our look at Luis' outstanding career to date, we review the incredible impact he has had for his national team, from his debut for Uruguay in 2007 through to a dazzling triumph at the 2011 Copa America. And he hopes there's more to come...

LIKE any youngster, Luis Alberto Suarez Diaz always dreamt of representing his country. Those ambitions crystallised in the years after he moved from Salto to the capital city, Montevideo, at the age of 11.

Suarez moved away from home to join the ranks of one of the country's biggest teams, Nacional, and gradually worked his way into their first-team set-up in 2005/06.

After just one season, he was on the move again. Still a teenager, he headed further afield to try his luck in Europe by signing for Dutch side Groningen.

It was at this time that he first wore the national team colours, playing in four matches for Uruguay's Under 20s in 2006/2007 and scoring twice.

A focus on youth development led by national coach Oscar Tabarez led to raised standards at youth level. Suarez was quickly highlighted by Tabarez, nicknamed 'The Teacher' to be a part of the programme.

Suarez made a good start to his career in the Dutch Eredivisie and soon after his 20th birthday was called up to make his debut for the senior national team.

In keeping with what has so far been a colourful international career, Suarez made an eventful debut on February 8, 2007.

Uruguay defeated Colombia 3-1 in a friendly in Barranquilla but Suarez was sent off after collecting a second yellow card five minutes from time.

Just 15 minutes into the game, the striker had earned a penalty when he was upended by goalkeeper Miguel Calero, who was dismissed for the foul.

Suarez missed out on selection for the 2007 Copa America in Venezuela, a tournament which saw Uruguay reach the semi-finals before losing to Brazil on penalties.

They eventually finished fourth after being beaten by Mexico in the third place play-off.

However Suarez was back in the squad the following year by which time he had completed his move to Ajax. He scored his first senior goal for his country in a February 2008 friendly against Colombia at the Centenario Stadium, side-stepping goalkeeper Agustin Julio to slot home an 86th minute equaliser as the game ended 2-2.

Uruguay's next target was reaching the 2010 World Cup.

Luis always dreamt of playing for Uruguay, but now he is one of his country's footballing icons

>>

Suarez ensured their CONMEBOL qualification campaign started off on the right note by scoring the opening goal in a 5-0 defeat of Bolivia in Montevideo.

Following a 1-0 loss in Paraguay, Suarez struck again in La Celeste's next qualifier, a 2-2 draw with Chile, whose goals both came from the recalled veteran striker Marcelo Salas.

A 2-1 defeat in Brazil followed by a 1-1 home draw with Venezuela left Uruguay in a precarious position in their group. However, a 6-0 rout of Peru in their next match – with Diego Forlan scoring a hat-trick – put things back on track.

A 1-0 win in Colombia strengthened their position before a goalless draw with Ecuador earned them another point.

Diego Maradona's Argentina then overcame Uruguay 2-1 in Buenos Aires before a patched-up La Celeste came from two goals down to draw 2-2 with Bolivia in La Paz.

Next up was a home game against Paraguay with Suarez providing the assists for both goals in a 2-0 victory. But a goalless draw in Chile then preceded a disappointing 4-0 home reverse at the hands of Brazil.

And although Suarez was on target in a 2-2 draw in Venezuela, a 1-0 setback against Peru in Lima

SUAREZ, STANDING ON THE GOALLINE, TOOK A CALCULATED RISK AND PALMED THE BALL AWAY

left Uruguay in a difficult position again.

An early goal from Suarez helped his country to a 3-1 win over Colombia before another strike from Suarez and an injury-time penalty from Forlan kept their hopes up with a 2-1 win over Ecuador in Quito.

Uruguay's final qualifier saw them come up against Maradona's Argentina who needed a victory to assure themselves of qualification.

A late goal from substitute Mario Bolatti meant Argentina qualified automatically and forced Uruguay to enter the play-offs where they would face Concacaf side Costa Rica over two legs for the right to play in the finals the following summer.

A first half goal from captain Diego Lugano was enough to give them a narrow first leg win in Saprissa and a 1-1 draw back in Montevideo booked their place in the finals.

Suarez had been a regular in the Uruguay squad throughout the qualification process and was duly selected for the 23-man group for South Africa.

The tournament, dubbed the greatest show on earth, was to be one of the highlights of Suarez's career to date.

In the first phase, Tabarez's squad were grouped with France, South Africa and Mexico.

In their opening fixture, Uruguay held fancied France to a goalless draw in Cape Town. They then produced a polished performance to see off the host nation 3-0 in Pretoria.

Suarez shone as two goals from Forlan and a late strike by Alvaro Pereira left South Africa's hopes of reaching the knockout phase in the balance.

There were no such worries for Uruguay however and a first-half goal from Suarez against Mexico in Rustenburg in their final group game assured top spot in Group A.

The squad travelled to Port Elizabeth for their last 16 match against South Korea and Suarez struck twice to give his country a 2-1 win and a place in the World Cup quarter-finals for the first time since 1970. His clinical double took his tally for the season to 55 in 61 games.

Uruguay were paired with Ghana in the last eight and a crowd of more than 84,000 filed into the Soccer City Stadium in Johannesburg. They would witness what would be one of the games of the tournament with Suarez cast as one of the central characters in the drama which unfolded.

Sulley Muntari had given Ghana the lead with a long-range effort before Forlan drew Uruguay level with a well taken free-kick.

There was no further scoring and the game went into extra-time. As the additional period came to a close, Ghana ended strongly and they looked to have won the game when Dominic Adiyiah produced a goalbound header. Suarez, standing on the goalline, took a calculated risk and palmed the ball away.

He was immediately sent off but Asamoah Gyan's spot-kick hit the crossbar to take the tie to penalties.

Uruguay's subsequent shoot-out success handed them a semi-final date with Holland but the suspended Suarez had to watch from the sidelines.

His attacking menace was missed as Holland won 3-2 in Cape Town but Uruguay's achievement in reaching the final four of the tournament saw the squad hailed as heroes in their homeland.

"I'm very proud of my players," said coach Tabarez. "We went very far, no-one expected that, so that helps the sadness of the defeat."

Suarez's handball against Ghana had caused plenty of debate throughout footballing circles but the player received the full backing of his coach.

Talking about the incident, Tabarez said. "I

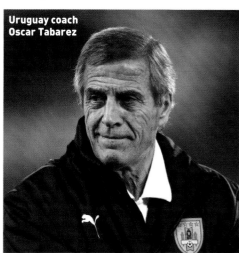

Uruguay coach Oscar Tabarez

Suarez and Diego Forlan celebrate success at the 2010 World Cup, although (below) Luis was sent off in the quarter-final against Ghana

>>

think it was instinctive. The player instinctively reacted and was thrown out of the match and he can't play the next match. What else do you want?

"Is Suarez also to blame for Ghana missing the penalty? We try to be dignified and if we lose a match we look for the reasons for it. You shouldn't look to third parties. This is football.

66 SUAREZ IS AN ELITE PLAYER IN WORLD FOOTBALL

There are consequences to that handball and he didn't know that Ghana was going to miss that penalty."

Suarez returned to the starting line-up for the third place play-off against Germany in Port Elizabeth which, like the semi-final, ended in a 3-2 defeat.

An entertaining game saw Uruguay come from behind to take the lead only to surrender it again in the final 10 minutes.

Overall, however, the tournament was a success for Suarez as he scored three goals in

six games and forged a potent partnership with Forlan in attack.

In the year since the World Cup he continued to be a key figure in the Uruguay set-up and scored his first international hat-trick last October during a 7-1 friendly win in Indonesia.

Suarez went into his first Copa America in the summer of 2011 with a record of 16 goals in 39 appearances for Uruguay. Before the tournament he told Liverpool's official club magazine of his pride at pulling on the sky blue shirt of his country.

"It means a lot for me. From being a child it is always your dream to play for your country and that's the case with everyone in Uruguay. To actually get the chance to achieve that ambition is fantastic.

"You know that by doing well in 90 minutes and playing really, really well you're bringing so much joy and happiness to people. The World Cup campaign that we managed to achieve is something that Uruguay hasn't done for so long so it was absolutely great that we brought a lot of joy to people with that campaign."

The Copa America would eclipse those achievements and Suarez's star had never been brighter than when it shone so dazzlingly during the competition held in Argentina.

He was voted the Most Valuable Player in the Copa America after firing his country to a record 15th success.

Razor-sharp throughout, his strike partnership with Forlan proved decisive and, but for a hat-trick by Peru striker Paolo Guerrero in the third-place play-off, he would also have finished with the golden boot.

He showed his worth as a key component in the Uruguayan attack during the early stages of the tournament.

He struck an equaliser in Uruguay's opening game against Peru and then produced a clever piece of play to provide an assist for Alvaro Pereira as Uruguay had to settle for another 1-1 draw with Chile in their second fixture.

A win against Mexico in the final group game ensured progress to the quarter-finals on what was a historic day in Uruguay's footballing history.

The last eight clash with Argentina in Santa Fe was played on July 16, the same day on which La Celeste had defeated Brazil to win the 1950 World Cup.

Despite playing more than half of the match with 10 men after Bologna's Diego Perez was sent off, Uruguay held on to draw 1-1 and after no further goals in extra-time, the tie was decided on penalties.

Suarez kept his calm to slot home his country's second spot-kick and with Carlos Tevez failing with his effort, Uruguay went on to win 5-4.

The striker said afterwards: "July 16 was a historic date, and we talked about it, and we also wanted to make history.

"It's an incredible moment. I believe we deserved it because in the first half 'the Russian' [Perez] was sent off, and justice was served.

"We knew playing against the hosts was going

Forlan and Suarez have
been a potent force for
their country as they have
risen up the world rankings

>> to be difficult because we had all of the
stadium against us, but we have to thank all
of the fans and family who came to support
us."

The shoot-out success set up a semi-final
showdown with Peru in La Plata with Suarez
again stealing the show with two second-half
goals to book Uruguay's place in the final.

First he scored from an acute angle.
Minutes later he cleverly rounded Fernandez
before stroking the ball into an empty net.

Coach Tabarez did not hold back in his
praise for the man in the number nine shirt.

"He (Suarez) is an elite player in world
football," he said. "We talked about having
more presence up top. That is how we got
the first goal. (Diego) Forlan and Suarez
appeared. After that, Peru kept attacking, but
we had it under control."

Suarez's brace put him joint top of
the Copa goalscoring charts and booked
Uruguay's passage into the final against
Paraguay in Buenos Aires.

That's when a memorable tournament
turned into a defining point in Suarez's
career.

His 11th minute goal was added to by a
Forlan brace for a 3-0 victory.

Becoming a champion of his continent
surpassed the previous summer's
achievements at the World Cup and the
personal accolades were heartening too.

Reflecting on his successes, Suarez told
LFC magazine: "As you can imagine for me
as a Uruguayan it was a very proud moment.
I think it was something that the whole
country had been looking forward to and it
now gives us something to build on for the
future as well.

"On a personal level, the (MVP) award was
a nice extra prize and it made me very happy
but I'm more interested in the team getting
the awards than personal honours.

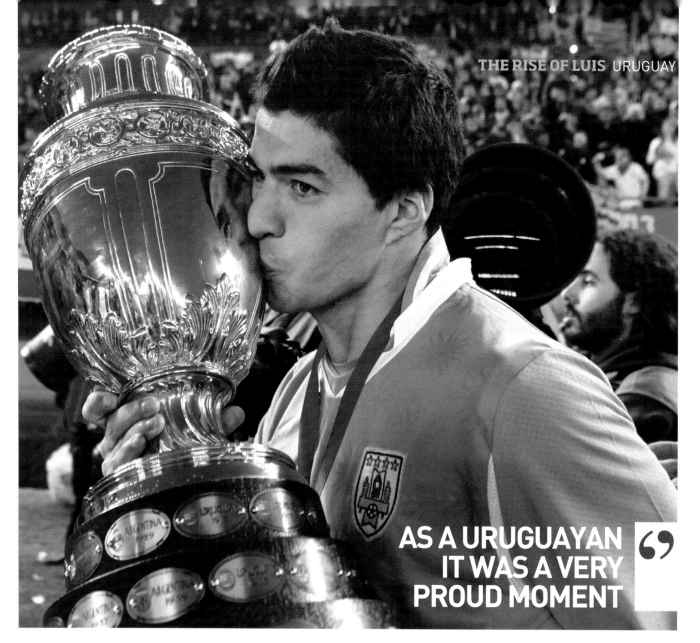

AS A URUGUAYAN IT WAS A VERY PROUD MOMENT

Suarez kisses the trophy as his country landed the Copa America in 2011

"It gave us the chance to show Uruguayans that we had gone back to the Uruguay of old who used to dominate world football. I think the way that the team played also made them very, very proud. And also the fact that Uruguay is such a small country (with a population of around 3.5 million). For them to now be amongst the best in the world is something super special."

Looking back at his country's triumph, he says there were two main personal highlights. First was that quarter-final against Argentina in Santa Fe which saw Uruguay win on penalties after being reduced to 10 men. Second, of course, was the final itself.

"The victory against Argentina was a highlight," he says. "On the one hand there were the circumstances as we were playing with one man less for some time. On the other to beat the host nation, even on penalties, was special. And, of course, winning the final was very important for me.

"I was very grateful for the backing that I received from the people at home and also here (in Liverpool) but also the support of my family, my wife and child. They were there watching me all the time and had to put up with long trips between games and looking after everything. Even things like looking after food for the baby was a bit different so I was very grateful for the support that they gave in quite difficult circumstances."

Asked if the Copa triumph represented the best moment of his career so far, Suarez, still only 24, intimated his hope there will be more to come.

"I think it's a bit early to be talking about best moments in my career as I am still quite young," he said. "But certainly the final of the Copa America was probably the best so far on a personal level and also on a national level as well."

He continued his fine form with the national team into the opening qualifiers for the 2014 World Cup, finding the net in Uruguay's opening match against Bolivia in Montevideo.

Suarez says that as they focus on reaching the finals in Brazil, it is vital that the team puts their summer exploits behind them.

He says: "It's really important for Uruguay to forget about the 2010 World Cup and also the Copa America now and think about the 2014 World Cup and hopefully get the team playing the way they have been again."

STATS

Copa America

Games: 6
Goals: 4
Assists: 1
Shots: 15
Shots on target: 7
Fouls committed: 11
Fouls against: 28
Yellow cards: 2
Red cards: 0

Source: ESPN soccernet

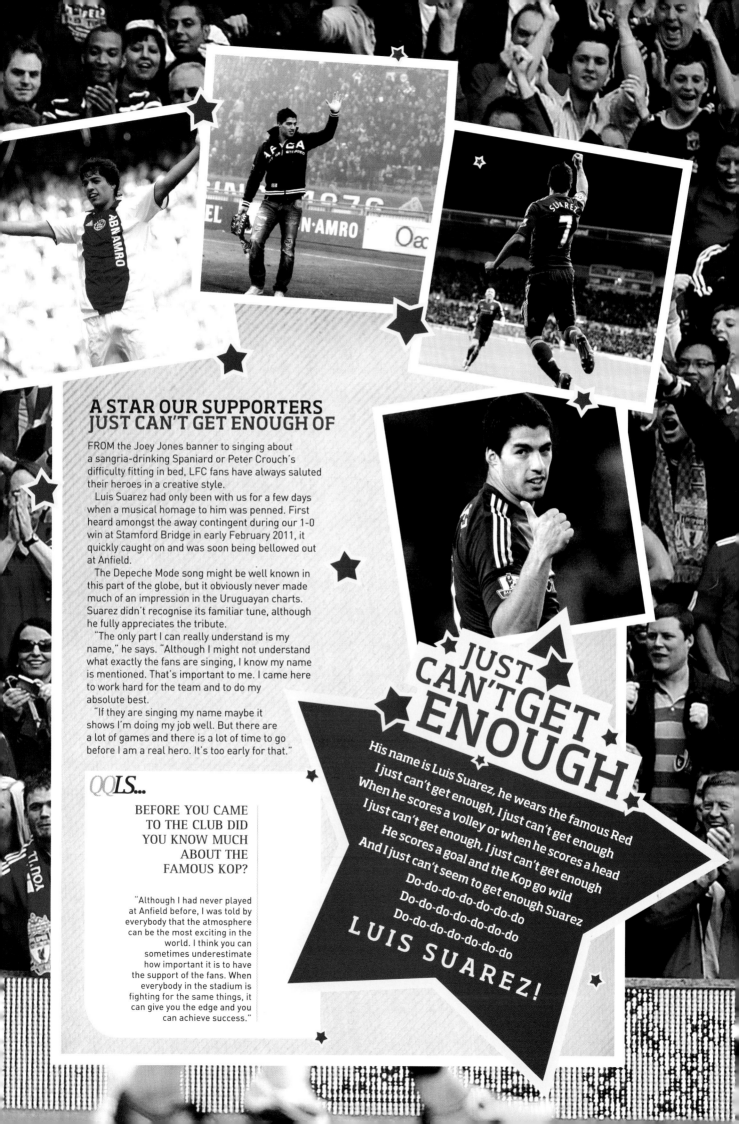

A STAR OUR SUPPORTERS JUST CAN'T GET ENOUGH OF

FROM the Joey Jones banner to singing about a sangria-drinking Spaniard or Peter Crouch's difficulty fitting in bed, LFC fans have always saluted their heroes in a creative style.

Luis Suarez had only been with us for a few days when a musical homage to him was penned. First heard amongst the away contingent during our 1-0 win at Stamford Bridge in early February 2011, it quickly caught on and was soon being bellowed out at Anfield.

The Depeche Mode song might be well known in this part of the globe, but it obviously never made much of an impression in the Uruguayan charts. Suarez didn't recognise its familiar tune, although he fully appreciates the tribute.

"The only part I can really understand is my name," he says. "Although I might not understand what exactly the fans are singing, I know my name is mentioned. That's important to me. I came here to work hard for the team and to do my absolute best.

"If they are singing my name maybe it shows I'm doing my job well. But there are a lot of games and there is a lot of time to go before I am a real hero. It's too early for that."

QQLS...

BEFORE YOU CAME TO THE CLUB DID YOU KNOW MUCH ABOUT THE FAMOUS KOP?

"Although I had never played at Anfield before, I was told by everybody that the atmosphere can be the most exciting in the world. I think you can sometimes underestimate how important it is to have the support of the fans. When everybody in the stadium is fighting for the same things, it can give you the edge and you can achieve success."

JUST CAN'T GET ENOUGH

His name is Luis Suarez, he wears the famous Red
I just can't get enough, when he scores a volley or when he scores a head
I just can't get enough, when he scores a head
I just can't get enough, I just can't get enough
He scores a goal and the Kop go wild
And I just can't seem to get enough Suarez
Do-do-do-do-do-do-do
Do-do-do-do-do-do-do
Do-do-do-do-do-do-do

LUIS SUAREZ!

ON MAKING LIFE
DIFFICULT FOR DEFENDERS

V ARSENAL

20.08.2011

"I feel no pressure at all. In fact when a defender studies you, it almost makes it easier because you just don't do what he expects you to. If he thinks you are going to go to your right, you go to your left and so on and you just keep switching it round so you are hard to read. It keeps you on your toes but really it's harder for the defender because he can't know what you are going to do."

What they said about him...

"The more I see of Luis Suarez the more he reminds me of Kevin Keegan. His movement is exceptional and Suarez is a fine player.
    "He doesn't just have the ability to beat someone for pace, he can stop, stand on the ball and then nutmeg you.
    "He has great skill and plays the game in areas where defenders don't like it."

TOMMY SMITH

On similarities with Kevin Keegan

"I have spoken to Luis. He got in touch with me and we had a chat. It is good there is another Uruguayan already in the team - it is easier if there is someone I know well.
    "He has told me what the club is like. It's important because he won over the fans straight away and is scoring goals. He's doing really well, and that's good for me as another Uruguayan arriving."

SEBASTIAN COATES

Prior to arriving at Anfield

"The movement Luis has is unreal. You know what you are going to get from him in every game, whether it be a Barclays Premier League game or a Carling Cup tie.
    "He was brilliant again for us. He makes our job easier and if he keeps doing that for the rest of the season then I think him and Andy are going to cause defenders and teams a lot of problems."

JAY SPEARING

After the Exeter Carling Cup game

"Suarez is a fantastic player. He has settled in brilliantly to the Premier League and I can't wait to play alongside him. I remember my first pre-season at Sunderland under Steve Bruce and I first saw him play in the Amsterdam Tournament and he was brilliant."

JORDAN HENDERSON

On the first time he saw Luis play

"Luis is special. His movement, his touch, his awareness and the way he takes his goals is fantastic.
    "I think he is sensational and it's great to play with him. He's a midfielder's dream and he is only going to get better this season."

STEVEN GERRARD

August 2011

"I think if they can gel, which they should be able to, the partnership between Carroll and Suarez could be a really big thing.

"It doesn't matter that they are from different backgrounds. Actually, Kenny and I didn't speak much off the pitch.

"I talk to him far more now than I ever did when we were playing together. We just fitted in because we had different skills.

"I had speed and could finish chances, and he had the most amazing football brain.

"I've watched Andy getting his fitness up to standard on the club's Far East tour and when Suarez gets back from international duty and the two start training together, I'm sure they'll build up a partnership.

"The potential is fantastic. Andy came to us with injuries last season, but in any case your first spell at a club like Liverpool is always an adjustment.

"People forget that I struggled a bit in my first season. But I've no doubt it will come right for him - and quickly, too."

IAN RUSH On Andy Carroll and Luis Suarez partnership in July 2011

"When he gets the ball you never know what he is going to do. Suarez always shows a desire to get forward, to do something different. He plays the kind of football fans want to watch.

"Since he's come here, he's really took to it - probably better than most foreign players. He's settled instantly. He'll be a huge player for the club over the next few years."

STEWART DOWNING
Why Suarez is so hard to stop

"Lots of people have arrived at Liverpool and people have said they remind me of Dalglish - and they never were because he was so special, but Suarez might just be the closest.

"He's got all the ability in the world and a real mean streak. He is a top player.

"Kenny's eyes light up when he talks about him. He's got that little bit of everything and when you see goals like he scored at Sunderland last season you ask yourself 'how's he done that?', which was another trait Dalglish had.

"He's got great ability. He is very aware of everything, a real team player a handful to play against and like all South Americans can really look after himself. Players like Diego Maradona and Carlos Tevez found themselves getting booted on a regular basis but were tough and could give it back. Suarez is the same."

MARK LAWRENSON
Why Suarez is the real deal

GREAT SUAREZ GAMES

LUIS SUAREZ DOESN'T HAVE TO SCORE GOALS TO LEAVE A LASTING IMPRESSION ON A GAME. HE SPRINKLES HIS MAGIC OVER EVERY MATCH HE PLAYS IN. HERE'S A REMINDER OF SOME OF HIS BEST GAMES IN A LIVERPOOL SHIRT SO FAR

LIVERPOOL 3
MANCHESTER UNITED 1
Premier League
Anfield, 06/03/11

THIS game saw Suarez establish himself as a firm favourite with Kopites.

Dirk Kuyt may have made the headlines with a hat-trick but Suarez tormented the United defence with a stunning display of his repertoire. He slalomed his way past Rafael, Michael Carrick and Wes Brown to put the opening goal on a plate for Kuyt.

The second goal stemmed from a Suarez cross that Nani failed to clear and the third from a free-kick from the Uruguayan which proved too hot for Edwin van der Sar to handle.

In short United couldn't cope with Suarez who helped the Reds celebrate Kenny Dalglish's 60th birthday - two days earlier - in style.

SUNDERLAND 0
LIVERPOOL 2
Premier League
Stadium of Light, 20/03/11

ONE of the highlights of Liverpool's win in Wearside was Suarez's stunning goal that put the seal on a 2-0 success.

As was so often the case during his first half-season with the club, opposing defences found it difficult to cope with Suarez's clever link-up play and movement.

He had one effort palmed away by goalkeeper Simon Mignolet before wriggling his way along the by-line to beat the Belgian from an acute angle for the Reds' brilliant second.

His constant movement proved too much for the home side, who had defender John Mensah sent off later on for hauling down the Uruguayan.

FULHAM 2
LIVERPOOL 5
Premier League
Craven Cottage, 09/05/11

MAXI Rodriguez grabbed his second hat-trick in the space of a couple of weeks as Suarez wreaked havoc in the Monday evening early summer sunshine down by the Thames.

The strong, quicksilver attacker showed strength in holding the ball up and immense skill in wriggling his way free of defenders during an eye-catching performance.

At times he was simply unplayable as the Reds produced some of their best football of the season.

Suarez finally grabbed the goal he deserved, Liverpool's fifth, when he nonchalantly rounded goalkeeper Mark Schwarzer before tapping into an empty net.

LIVERPOOL 1
SUNDERLAND 1
Premier League
Anfield, 13/08/11

FOLLOWING his Copa America triumph with Uruguay, Suarez had only been back at Melwood five days before the Reds' opening game of the league season.

Some fans speculated that he might not figure at all but they were given a boost when he was named in the starting line-up for the clash with Steve Bruce's side.

It wasn't long before he was in the action, winning a penalty as he was tripped by Kieran Richardson as he bore down on goal.

He skied the penalty high over the bar but showed his strength of personality by stooping to head home a Charlie Adam free-kick soon afterwards.

LIVERPOOL 3
BOLTON WANDERERS 1
Premier League
Anfield, 27/08/11

ONCE again, Suarez played a starring role as the Reds saw off the challenge of Bolton.

Opposing central defenders Gary Cahill and Zat Knight endured difficult afternoons as the Reds produced some attractive inter-play in and around the visitors' box.

One breathtaking combination in the second half involved a series of short passes between Stewart Downing, Suarez, Jose Enrique and Dirk Kuyt which eventually led to Suarez rounding the keeper but hitting the side-netting.

Although Suarez didn't get on the scoresheet himself, he played a part in the third goal for Charlie Adam and was generally a menace to the Bolton back line.

LIVERPOOL 2
WOLVES 1
Premier League
Anfield, 24/09/11

A MESMERISING display which had the Wolves defence tied in knots for large periods of the game. Suarez showcased his sublime skills with another highly entertaining all-action performance.

A constant threat to centre-backs Roger Johnson and Christophe Berra, Suarez's man of the match performance was defined by a brilliant goal that gave Liverpool a two-goal advantage at half-time.

Among the many other highlights in the 82 minutes he was on the pitch were an outrageous turn to fox Roger Johnson and another fine piece of trickery on the by-line which almost teed up Andy Carroll.

EVERTON 0
LIVERPOOL 2
Premier League
Goodison Park, 01/10/11

SUAREZ'S first experience of the Merseyside derby was a winning one and, as always, he was at the heart of the action.

The Reds' number seven was involved in the incidents which saw Jack Rodwell sent off midway through the first half and Phil Jagielka concede a penalty.

After the break, Suarez continued to prove a handful for the Everton defence, scoring the Reds' second goal in front of the Gwladys Street after causing confusion between Jagielka and Leighton Baines.

He almost provided an assist in added time too, with a clever corner which resulted in Dirk Kuyt clipping the post.

The Melwood Magician

THE tricks and skills Luis Suarez displays in every match come largely from a creative and alert mind that transforms quick thoughts into amazing pieces of individual brilliance.

You don't get anywhere in life without hard work though, and Melwood is where our tricky Uruguayan puts in the hours to improve on a daily basis...and occasionally have a laugh too.

QQLS...

WHY DID YOU FEEL IT WAS IMPORTANT TO RETURN TO LIVERPOOL SO QUICKLY AFTER YOUR COPA AMERICA SUCCESS IN THE SUMMER OF 2011?

"I want to play in all the games I can for Liverpool. I don't want any rest at all. Despite only having that week's training before playing again, I'm only 24 so I felt good. I was glad to get back to training at Melwood as I had been missing that whole atmosphere around the training ground and wanted to get back to playing at Anfield. So it was really special for me to get back."

ON WINNING
THE COPA AMERICA

V PARAGUAY
24.07.2011

"We have a huge joy to give this title to our people. This is an indescribable feeling. We played as a group. I think when groups are united like this, everyone together and going for the same thing, you can get things done.
The important thing was getting started well. With two goals in the first half, I think it was very difficult for them to come back. Luckily, we reached the goal of getting to the final, which was what we wanted, and winning the title is the maximum you can get."

Perfect route to Euro success

SIMON HUGHES SPEAKS TO SOUTH AMERICAN FOOTBALL EXPERT **TIM VICKERY** TO GET HIS VIEWS ON EL PISTOLERO

SH: When Liverpool signed Luis Suarez, did you initially believe it was good business?

TV: Definitely. Given that he had only recently turned 24 he had huge potential to be an integral part of the Liverpool team for several years. Having been in Holland since 2006, he was ready for the step up. I think his time in the Eredivisie smoothed the transition towards being comfortable with the Premier League because in the past we have seen players come from South America and straight to a big club before failing. People argued this with Diego Forlan at Manchester United who since moving on from Old Trafford has proven to be an excellent player, but while in England was very much derided. When United brought him over from Independiente, he hadn't even played for Uruguay or in the Copa Libertadores. The move from South America to one of the big English clubs was too much too soon. The case of Suarez is different – he was an established international with experience of several years of European football behind him.

The move from Dutch football to English football is big but Suarez was ready for it.

SH: Do you remember the first time you saw him play for Nacional and how has he developed since then?

TV: He was first involved in the first-team aged 17 in 2005. There was a fuss about him straight away. The first thing that struck me and a lot of other people was the way he used his body strength to back into people – like the way Kenny Dalglish used to for Liverpool. He was brilliant with his back to goal, protecting the ball. If you can do that at 17 in a ruthless league like the Uruguayan Primera Division you know there is something special about the player. Nacional were fully aware of his talent and they appreciated that soon enough he'd be moving on. Back in 2005, Flamengo – the most popular club not just in Brazil but the whole of South America – were very interested in taking him to Rio. Instead, he ended up in Europe.

> "Suarez has so many tricks in his locker and will come at you with pace and strength. When on form he can be unstoppable"

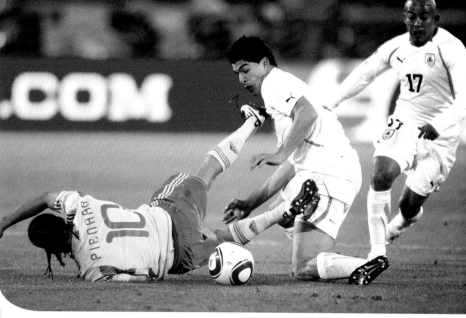

SH: What was his relationship with the Nacional fans like?

TV: He was only there in the first-team for a year before being swept away elsewhere but they were very excited about the player's potential. Uruguayan fans are now familiar with the process of their best young players being taken abroad because the country and its football teams just don't have the money to keep up with other leagues in South America – never mind Europe. Many Uruguayans quickly move to Spain, Italy or quite often Mexico six months after their first-team debut because it financially suits the club as well as the player. What people should appreciate is that Nacional are one of the two biggest clubs in Uruguay and expectations there are instant. Their city rivalry with Penarol is the oldest in the world outside Britain and they have squabbled about everything for more than 100 years. Nacional have a history in the Copa Libertadores but haven't won it since 1988. There is a weight of tradition attached straight away when any player makes his debut for Nacional – even if they aren't what they were - and Suarez dealt comfortably with that.

SH: How did international football aid his development?

TV: In South America, the Under-20 Championships and the World Youth Cup are very important competitions. He excelled in both and was promoted straight from the Under-20 team to the senior side just as they were trying to qualify for the World Cup in South Africa. Again, he dealt with that step up very, very well. The South American qualifiers are the real deal and are probably the most difficult continent to progress from because there are no easy games. I think we saw how competitive the South American qualifiers are by how well its qualifiers did last summer. As a 20-year-old it was a seamless transition for Suarez – he dealt with everything that was asked of him and soon started to score. His goal record at international level now stands with the best in the world – 16 in 30-odd appearances.

SH: Where do you see his strongest position?

TV: He's always been a striker whose best work is in the channels, drifting over to either wing. That is not to say that he doesn't have the single-mindedness of a central striker because he certainly does. For Uruguay, he has mainly started wide right, drifting inside. It makes him a real handful for defenders because his movement is clever and unpredictable. He is comfortable going inside or outside the defender and in some ways, moves like a latter-day Chris Waddle in terms of his footwork – although they are different in size and direct position. Suarez has so many tricks in his locker and will come at you with pace and strength. When on form – and those days were pretty frequent at Ajax – he can be unstoppable.

SH: Were you surprised when Suarez opted to move to Holland with a relatively small club in Groningen?

TV: In some ways, no. It was a sensible move that would aid him in the long-term. By going there,

he could settle into a new country without the instant expectation. That pressure came later with his move to Ajax. I would imagine Nacional were surprised more than most because Groningen wasn't necessarily the most expensive move on the table both for the club and the player. I think that in itself proves that he has the right people advising him. It was a sensible career move.

SH: How important was Suarez to Uruguay's World Cup campaign in 2010?

TV: He gave pace up front, fire and three goals. He was extremely important because they had a problem from the off finding a traditional number 10 – the playmaker. They knew they had the Suarez-Forlan combination and that proved dangerous all the way through the qualifiers. At home against weak sides, Uruguay really steamrollered past them because of the strikeforce. Yet the question remained – who would consistently provide the passes against the better opposition for them to score? They started off the first game with Nacho Gonzalez, who a few years ago had a short but controversial spell with Newcastle. That didn't work against France so they brought on Nicolas Lodeiro – Uruguay's big hope as a playmaker. Then he gets himself sent off. The only option left was to play Forlan a little bit deeper. It turned out to be a masterstroke – yet it was only successful because they still had Suarez and his pace and movement ahead of him.

SH: Is Suarez comfortable adjusting to different formations?

TV: When the current Uruguay coach Oscar Washington Tabarez took over he had a big masterplan to play the traditional 4-3-3. All of the youth teams would follow suit because it was the historical identity of Uruguayan football. It lasted exactly 90 minutes because they got whacked against Peru in the opening game of the Copa America playing that formation. Tabarez realised that he had to adapt the system to his best players. Uruguay became very flexible and in one of the qualifying games they desperately needed to win against Colombia in Bogota, so they played an old-style 4-2-4. Following that, they played with back threes, back fours and all kinds of different attacking shapes. Suarez played in nearly every game and has adapted very well to each situation. The telling statistic from the World Cup was that they had less possession in every game but more shots. Suarez was the one doing a lot of the shooting and gave Uruguay the opportunity to counter-attack with his pace.

SUAREZ STATS

Name:	LUIS SUAREZ
Born:	24 JAN, 1987
Height:	5FT 11IN (1.8M)
Weight:	12ST 7LB (79KG)
Place of birth:	SALTO, URUGUAY
Nationality:	URUGUAYAN
Date signed:	31 JAN, 2011
Squad number:	7

CAREER SO FAR...

CLUB	FROM	TO	LEAGUE APPS	GLS	FA CUP APPS	GLS	LGE CUP APPS	GLS	OTHER APPS	GLS
Liverpool	31 Jan, 11		20 (2)	8	0 (0)	0	3 (0)	3	0 (0)	0
Ajax	01 Jul, 07	31 Jan, 11	110 (0)	81	12 (0)	12	0 (0)	0	37 (0)	18
FC Groningen	01 Jul, 06	01 Jul, 07	29 (0)	10	2 (0)	1	0 (0)	0	6 (0)	4
Nacional (Uru)	01 Jul, 05	01 Jul, 06	27 (0)	10	0 (0)	0	0 (0)	0	7 (0)	2
Totals			186 (2)	109	14 (0)	13	3 (0)	3	50 (0)	24
Goals per Game			0.57		0.92		1.0		0.48	

All stats and information is correct up to 28.10.2011

GOALS

SEASON 2011/12
12 GAMES
7 GOALS

SEASON 2010/11
13 GAMES
4 GOALS

ASSISTS

SEASON 2011/12
12 GAMES
3 ASSISTS

SEASON 2010/11
13 GAMES
5 ASSISTS

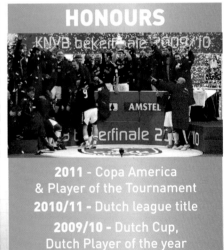

HONOURS

2011 - Copa America & Player of the Tournament
2010/11 - Dutch league title
2009/10 - Dutch Cup, Dutch Player of the year
2005/06 - Uruguayan league title

Answers from Suarez quiz on page 51 - 1. Ajax 2. Salto 3. El Pistolero 4. Paraguay 5. Exeter City 6. Robbie Keane 7. Enter our competition and tell us!